D0167156

THE PSYCHOLOGY
OF CHRISTIAN
EXPERIENCE

THE 'CONTEMPORARY EVANGELICAL PERSPECTIVES' SERIES

The Family in Dialogue   A. Donald Bell

Witness and Revelation in the Gospel of John   James M. Boice

The Protest of a Troubled Protestant   Harold O. J. Brown

A Shorter Life of Christ   Donald Guthrie

Inspiration and Canonicity of the Bible   R. Laird Harris

Christianity in a Revolutionary Age
(5-volume set)   Kenneth Scott Latourette

A History of the Expansion of Christianity
(7-volume set)   Kenneth Scott Latourette

An Evangelical Theology of Missions   Harold Lindsell

The Work of Christ   I. Howard Marshall

The Psychology of Christian Experience   W. Curry Mavis

Jesus—Human and Divine   H. D. McDonald

Saturation Evangelism   George W. Peters

God, the Atom and the Universe   James Reid

The Holy Spirit and His Gifts   J. Oswald Sanders

The Bible—the Living Word of Revelation   Merrill C. Tenney

Heredity   William J. Tinkle

Effective Bible Study   Howard F. Vos

The "Contemporary Evangelical Perspectives" Series

THE PSYCHOLOGY OF CHRISTIAN EXPERIENCE

by

W. CURRY MAVIS, Ph.D.

Department of Pastoral Work
Asbury Theological Seminary

ZONDERVAN
PUBLISHING HOUSE
OF THE ZONDERVAN CORPORATION | GRAND RAPIDS, MICHIGAN 49506

THE PSYCHOLOGY OF CHRISTIAN EXPERIENCE
Copyright 1963 by Zondervan Publishing House
Grand Rapids, Michigan

Library of Congress Catalog Card Number 63-9312

First printing 1963
Second printing 1964
Third printing 1969
Fourth printing 1970
Fifth printing 1972
Sixth printing 1973
Seventh printing 1974

Printed in the United States of America

PREFACE

Our generation needs voices that "speak eternal truth in its own dialect." The dialect of our age is strongly psychological and people interpret their experiences in the light of psychology. In seeking to speak to the present age, this book interprets some of the basic aspects of the Christian life with the help of valid psychological concepts. Thus, in the broadest sense, it may be thought of as a work in the psychology of Christian experience.

This volume devotes attention to personal religious living from the early awakening insights of spiritual need to the mature Christian life. First, it re-examines the nature of repentance, the new birth, spiritual cleansing, and assurance. Second, it devotes attention to principles and methods of maintaining virile spiritual health. In doing this it gives specific thought to the problems of personal maladjustment and their relationship to the Christian life. Third, it considers the psychological-spiritual climate of the present age and it discusses principles of effective and productive Christian living in such a generation.

This book emphasizes the importance of personal insight in the Christian life. Today's Christian needs to have a good understanding of human nature. He needs to know about the dynamics of human personality — the needs, interests, and urges of his own self. An understanding of human personality also contributes to a knowledge of the Christian way of life. The plan of salvation is God's response to human need.

The primary purpose of this work is to help people deepen their personal religious living through an increased knowledge of self and an enlarged understanding of the principles of the Christian life. The author believes that there is a growing awareness that our age demands a new quality of personal living. Our society has created new temptations and frustrations. There are new ways to be lost today, in addition to the old ways. There are powerful social forces that threaten both personal and corporate morality. Individual persons and society can be saved only by spiritual renewal. We must rediscover the great spiritual resources of life.

There are those in our day who believe deeply that their greatest potential for happiness and personal effectiveness lies in their undeveloped spiritual capacities. They think that progress in the development of character must keep up with the development of science an technology. On the international scene, they believe that it is better for us to outlive our potential enemies than to out-fight them. These people believe that personal spiritual living is a redemptive force in society and they have set out on a spiritual quest. This book is for them.

W. C. MAVIS

TABLE OF CONTENTS

PREFACE

PART ONE

BECOMING A CHRISTIAN

I. LOOKING AT VARIETIES OF REPENTANCE.......... 11
   Substitutes for Repentance................... 12
   Ambivalent Repentance 16
   Redemptive Repentance 19
II. KNOWING GOD'S CREATIVE POWER.............. 24
   The Creative Power of Divine Forgiveness..... 26
   The Creation of New Spiritual Dynamics...... 28
III. MOVING TOWARD MATURITY................... 34
   Human Commitment 36
   Divine Cleansing 38
IV. LIVING WITH CONFIDENCE..................... 44
   The Content of Christian Assurance........... 45
   Christian Assurance and Psychic Needs........ 49

PART TWO

KEEPING SPIRITUALLY FIT

V. UNDERSTANDING MALADJUSTIVE IMPULSES 59
   Acknowledging the Complexes............... 59
   Seeking Insight 63
   Recognizing Spiritual Drag.................. 66
   Promoting Christian Maturity................ 68
VI. LOOKING AT SPIRITUAL FRUSTRATIONS........... 73
   The Body: Friend or Foe?................... 73
   Temptation: Victory or Defeat?............. 78

VII. CULTIVATING THE CHRISTIAN LIFE.............. 82
    Knowing the Textbook..................... 82
    Personalizing Corporate Worship............. 86
    Making Private Prayer Creative............. 90
VIII. MAINTAINING HEALTHFUL ATTITUDES 96
    Keeping an Attitude of Personal Responsibility.. 96
    Conserving Energy Through Sincerity......... 98
    Advancing Through Aspiration...............101

PART THREE

LIVING MATURELY

IX. LIVING IN SECULAR DAYS......................107
    The Psychology of Secularism...............109
    Inverted Values.........................114
X. DEVELOPING FAITH CAPACITY...................118
    Conditioning Factors of Faith...............118
    A Curriculum for Building Faith.............123
XI. PERCEIVING GOD'S GUIDANCE...................128
    Maintaining Receptive Attitudes 128
    Using Approved Methods...................133
XII. DEMONSTRATING DYNAMIC CHRISTIAN LOVE......139
    Admirers of Christ.......................139
    Love That Motivates......................142
Bibliography 149
Index 153

Part I
Becoming a Christian

CHAPTER I

Looking at Varieties of Repentance

David Gray, a young Scottish poet, wrote to his parents after he had fallen sick with tuberculosis and had spent many weary and frustrating months in London. "Dear Parents: I am coming home. . . . I have come through things . . . that I shall never tell anyone but you. . . . O home, home, home." Young Gray expressed a normal human desire. He wanted to be at home in a time of trouble.

It seems that the human race maintains a similar attitude toward God. Men often have urges to return to their Heavenly Father in times of difficulty. Perhaps the desire to turn to God is latent always in every man. It is seen sometimes vividly in persons who appear to have little desire for religious matters.

Harry Milton Taylor tells of an incident in the Florida State Prison that emphasizes man's urge to return to God. For several years an Easter pageant, *Christus,* was performed in the prison. In one of the scenes, Judas threw himself before the cross in seeming repentance with the cry, "My Lord and my God, have mercy." The prisoners responded with such uninhibited cheering and enthusiasm at that point that the scene was withdrawn from the play. At the insistence of the prisoners, the scene was subsequently restored and an effort was made to control the response of the audience by a sign which read "No Response." The prisoners, having identified with Judas, gave a moving expression to a deeply rooted desire to return to God.

The idea of making a turn in the direction of life is prominent in the concept of repentance. An Old Testament word for repentance, *shûv*, literally means "to turn" or "to return." The most profound of the New Testament words for repentance, *metanoía*, suggests the same idea. It means literally "a change of mind," thus a turning in the psychological and spiritual direction of life. Repentance is a central term in the New Testament. It is a profound Biblical concept that appears often.

It must be recognized clearly, however, that the human desire for repentance does not assure a genuine return to God. This desire is resisted often by obstinate forces in personality. At times, the resisting forces frustrate the disposition to repent and the would-be penitent makes substitutes for repentance. This is a type of *pseudo* repentance. It is false and spurious, a deceptive resemblance of the genuine. In fact, it is no repentance at all. Secondly, the resisting forces sometimes effect a compromised settlement with God. This is a type of *ambivalent* repentance, a halfhearted return to the Father. Finally, the desire for repentance frequently overcomes the resisting forces, by the grace of God, and the penitent makes peace with his Maker. This is *redemptive* repentance.

SUBSTITUTES FOR REPENTANCE

Man has a deep-seated disposition to try to make substitutes for genuine repentance. Substitute activities and attitudes are offered God in lieu of repentance. This is usually done without a realization that one is seeking salvation on his own terms. The process works with varying degrees of "success." At least to a small degree, it usually reduces the spiritual discomfort that arises out of a convictive sense of sin. The would-be penitent comes to believe that he has squared things with God by giving Him a number of "good" things.

First, psychological *compensation* is an age-old substitute for genuine repentance. Compensation is a psychological process, largely unconscious, in which a person undertakes to cover up or disguise a personally unacceptable condition or trait by doing some good and desirable thing. In this connection, it is doing religious acts in order to avoid an authentic return to God. It is not outright hypocrisy; it is not a deliberate outward show to convince others of religiosity. It is primarily an effort to convince oneself that he is right with God.

Jesus knew that the human mind, in its resistance to genuine repentance, seeks to save face by compensatory activities. He reproved the Scribes and Pharisees in the most severe terms for saying long prayers as a substitute for their exploitative business practices (Luke 20:47). He upbraided them for neglecting judgment, mercy, and faith and for, as a compensation, scrupulously tithing the smaller garden vegetables, mint, anise, and cummin (Matthew 23:23, 24). With the finest of insight, Jesus told the religious leaders of His day that they flagrantly refused to follow God's will as revealed by prophets and righteous men but, as a substitute, they built tombs for the prophets and adorned the monuments of the righteous (Matthew 23:29-36).

The present practices of psychological compensation for spiritual failure are similar to those used when Jesus spoke to the religionists of His generation. There are those who affect a piety of life, while they withhold their love from God. Others give handsomely to the church, in order to feel more religious. Still others zealously engage in religion and in community service as a bid for God's favor.

A second type of substitution for genuine repentance is seen in the psychological process of *identification*. This is the process in which one seeks to justify himself before God by assuming that he has the traits of another person, or that he possesses the qualities of an institution to which he belongs. "In identification a person may regard as his own the achievements and qualities of others rather than face and constructively resolve his own conflicts."[1] The process is largely unconscious.

The Pharisees and Sadducees to whom John the Baptist preached, when confronted with a call to personal repentance, preferred not to change the direction of their lives. They "solved" their problem, reducing the tension, by identifying with Abraham. "We have Abraham to our Father." (Matthew 3:7-10). They believed that identity with Abraham's name justified them, righteous man that he was. In doing this, they committed a spiritual forgery. They sought to appropriate another man's spiritual merits by the use of his name. Saul of Tarsus resisted repentance by identification with his national religion, Judaism. As a leader in his religion, one confident of its validity, he carried on his ruthless deeds in the persecution of the earliest Christians.

Membership in Christian churches provides the most general method of psychological identification as a substitute for repentance. There are many who believe naively that they are Christians because they belong to a Christian church. They assume, subtly and half-consciously, that some of the virtues of the church are transferred automatically to them, by some means of spiritual wizardry. This assumption is due, in part, to the fact that sometimes the church approves them by accepting them as members though they have shown no turn in life direction. Thus they reason that God also approves them.

Thirdly, *symbolic words and acts* become substitutes for genuine repentance. The substitute word or act takes the place of a genuine attitude of turning to God. The words may be those in hallowed creeds or the acts may be the stately acts of reverential worship. The problem lies in the personal attitude toward and use of these valuable means.

The Hebrew prophets, with the clearest spiritual insight,

[1]Floyd Ruch, *Psychology and Life* (Chicago: Scott, Foresman and Co., 1953), p. 160.

portray God as uninterested in symbol-substitutes for righteous living.

> When you spread your hands,
> I will hide my eyes from you;
> even though you make many prayers,
> I will not listen;
> your hands are full of blood.
>
> (Isaiah 1:15, R.S.V.)

Jesus refused to accept reverential words as a substitute
for obedience. "And why call ye me, Lord, Lord, and do
not the things which I say?" (Luke 6:46).

Symbol-substitutes are still offered to God. Words of
repentance are substituted for works of righteousness. Litanies of consecration take the place of life commitments. The
saying of orthodox creeds displaces orthodox living. Loyalty
to religious traditions compensates for present loyalty to
Christ. The symbol-substitutes involve the most sacred
things of our faith. Baptism is sometimes substituted for
genuine spiritual renewal, and participation in the Lord's
supper takes the place of participation in the life of Christ.

To be more specific and detailed, an expression of sorrow
for sin is often made a substitute for an amendment of life.
There are many worshipers who stand in sacred precincts
on Sunday mornings from 11:00 A.M. to 12 NOON and tell
God how sorrowful they are because of their sins. They
assure God, in time-honored litanies, that they desire to
amend their lives. Some of these people, however, return
with delight to the sins they confessed, as soon as the benediction is said. This is verbal repentance, a word drama,
and an unproductive religious exercise. The worshiper
offered holy words to God without the sanction of his
inner self.

The habit of confessing sins, by word or act, without a
will to forsake them, is deadening spiritually. The practice
is a sedative to the soul. It tranquilizes the questing spirit.
The worshiper naively assumes, in such cases, that he has

found an expeditious way of handling his sin problem. He can follow the sinful ways of the world and yet right himself with heaven with a minimum of inconvenience.

One secures himself against genuine spiritual renewal when he adopts the substitution of religious words and acts for an inner change of mind. Virtue then consists of confessing sins and not in avoiding them. One develops a cold and insensitive heart, believing that God Himself cares little about righteous living inasmuch as He apparently accepts the substitution of sanctimonious words for right living. "The hardest sinner in all the whole lot," says Josh Billings, "is the one who spends half of his time sinning and the other half in repentance." Confession becomes a demonic substitution for genuine repentance if it lessens the impulse to righteous living.

AMBIVALENT REPENTANCE

Ambivalent repentance is halfhearted repentance. One part of the personality repents while another part remains impenitent. Some of the sentiments, attitudes, and ideas seek to turn to God while others cling to the old ways. In ambivalent repentance, certain sins are renounced, sometimes only academically, while others are embraced. The ambivalent penitent presumes to leave sin, but as Lot's wife, he looks back to his cherished interests. He seeks to make a compromised settlement of his life with God in which the Almighty receives certain areas for control while he himself retains others.

In ambivalent repentance one becomes religious by the addition of certain sacred ideas and practices rather than by a radical renunciation of all his evil ways. He comes to believe in the religious life as well as in the ways of the world, as the naive and frankly spoken little actress who said that she "believed in everything, a little bit." He becomes Christian partially on the basis of a conditioned

commitment. "I will follow thee; but let me first go . . ."
(Luke 9:61).

A conditioned commitment leads to a divided heart. Thus,
sentiments are a mixture of both sacred and worldly feelings.
Dispositions go in opposite directions. Interests center
around both positive and negative values. Ideas are basically contradictory, though frequently the contradiction is
unrecognized. There is a psychological and spiritual bi-
polarity with the sacred pulling in one direction and the
worldly in the other.

The man with a divided heart loves God and he also
resents Him. He esteems the eternal principles of righteousness, but he also has a practical regard for "realism." He
seeks to belong to both the Kingdom of God and the kingdom of this world.

Paul gives a superbly fine example of ambivalence in the
seventh chapter of Romans. He describes there a person,
perhaps himself before conversion, who wished to renounce
sin and to live righteously, but he found himself frustrated
and defeated by inner forces that opposed his good intentions. "So I find it to be a law that when I want to do right,
evil lies close at hand. For I delight in the law of God, in
my inmost self, but I see in my members another law at war
with the law of my mind and making me captive to the law
of sin which dwells in my members" (Romans 7:21-23,
R.S.V.). Paul was astounded at the ambivalence of his heart.
The contrary impulses seemed unthinkable to his real self.
In his vivid description he saw in his members another law,
really a "second me," that opposed his intention to live right
(Romans 8:23).

Goethe anticipated the psychological concept of ambivalent repentance in his description of the human mind possessed by a worldly spirit that opposed the high-minded and
spiritual urges.

Two spirits dwell at odds within my heart,
And each from the other would gladly part.
The one seems with a single urge possessed
To keep the friendly earth within my heart;
The other draws me forth in wilful quest
Of visions to an inner world apart.

Seneca, and other philosophers, have tried to describe human ambivalence by referring to "two souls" in man, one good and the other bad. They have said that life goes well when the good soul is in dominance but there is spiritual defeat and disorder when the bad soul is in control.

Ambivalent repentance arises out of contrary forces in human nature. Human nature itself constitutes an unfavorable situation for genuine repentance because so many of the feeling tones are unfriendly to a change in life. The emotions are not bystanders in the game of life, as benched players at a football game. They are eager participants, and they often resist the mind as it envisions values that can be attained only in the distant future. The emotions, in close relationship with the physical senses, have a short-time perspective. They want immediate satisfaction, as Passion in *Pilgrim's Progress*. Furthermore, they are usually reluctant to join the mind in resisting sin, particularly some of the varieties, because sin appeals strongly to the senses. The sensual appeal of sin has been primary since that first day when Adam and Eve found the fruit of the tree "a delight to the eyes" (Genesis 3:6, R.S.V.).

The contrary forces in human nature reduce one's ability to be decisive. Contrary attitudes argue for different decisions. Positive and negative impulses oppose each other. The tendency to approach is negated by the tendency to avoid. A neutrality is effected because the approach-avoidance factors balance each other and no decision is made for a change of life direction. The personality, as a committee with a tied vote, is inactive, is in a state of spiritual neutrality.

Sometimes this state of indecision is accounted for on the

basis of an "open mind," always a personally enhancing explanation. A true account would be on the basis of inner mental conflict that expends psychic and spiritual energy that should be used in decisive action.

The greatest problems in repentance for every man are seen in the ambivalence of human nature. The impulse to repent is opposed by contrary sentiments, attitudes, and dispositions. Rebellious impulses of the heart, loving the old ways of life, resist a change of direction. Few words in the English language describe human nature as well as the word, ambivalence. Few concepts give more insight into inner spiritual struggles.

Ambivalent repentance presents one of the major hazards in the spiritual quest. It has great power for self-deception. It tends to present a personally favorable, but basically false image to the would-be penitent. This is readily seen in the fact that every normal man wishes to see himself in the best light. The unscrupulous businessman looks at his deeds of benevolence instead of at his questionable business practices. He thus sees a good citizen benefiting society. The Pharisee looks to his pious practices rather than to his cold heart. He sees a man of righteousness. The concentration on the good and the suppression of the bad, are self-deceptive.

REDEMPTIVE REPENTANCE

Redemptive repentance is a genuine and wholehearted return to God. It involves an authentic change of mind concerning sin. It brings about a change of direction in life.

Redemptive repentance is one of the great reconstructive forces in human personality. It is the demonstration of the courage that it takes to see one's personal equation written out. It is a personal affirmation that the "unexamined life is not worth living." It is a dynamic approval of the proposition that "growth toward the best can only follow knowledge of the worst."[2] It is an adventure on the psychiatric insight that "It is only insofar as we admit our instincts that we can control and sublimate them."[3] It opens the door of the heart to the power of God.

Redemptive repentance is reconstructive because it is an implementation of personal insight. Man has seen his old spiritual furnishings, with the sins involved. Genuine repentance represents his self-conscious effort, by God's grace, to become a new man. It is a decision to defy the demons of the soul and to take positive action in reconstructing right relationships with God and one's self. It is a renunciation of the old sins and an invitation to the new life. It is a challenge to the heavy spiritual drag of the soul.

Redemptive repentance is turning about and facing God. It is a responsive approach toward God with a hand extended toward His as an entreaty for reconciliation. It is a farewell to the old ways and an invitation to new life. It is a call to the Almighty to transform attitudes, refine sentiments, create new ideals, and redirect old habits.

In redemptive repentance the sinner accepts responsibility for his spiritual disorder. He does not justify himself because of innate impulses that led him away from God. He does not condemn his environment, though he were reared on the wrong side of the tracks. He does not blame his parents who failed to understand him. He does not reproach his inheritance. He does not find fault with God for His pattern of man and the world. He does not seek to escape responsibility in rationalizing away the sinfulness of sin by considering it a type of moral prankishness. In spite of all the conditioning and extenuating factors, he accepts the final responsibility for his acts.

Redemptive repentance relates to the past, the present, and the future. It looks to the past in sorrow, earnestly be-

[2]Albert C. Outler, *Psychotherapy and the Christian Message* (New York: Harper and Bros., 1954), p. 170.
[3]J. A. Hadfield, *Psychology and Morals* (New York: R. M. McBride & Co., 1925), p. 189.

seeching God for the forgiveness of sins. It looks to the present in contrition because of an estranged and a sinful heart. The sinner not only acknowledges what he has done, but he confesses what he is, praying "God be merciful to me a sinner." Evil attitudes, sentiments, and ideals are renounced. Genuine repentance looks to the future with resolution and faith, with a commitment to God to live righteously by His strength.

Real repentance is redemptive because it is a pre-judgment appointment with God. It undertakes to reconstruct personality before it is too late. In the divine-human appointment, God and man work together in handling the sin problem. Man joins with the Almighty in condemning his sins and he turns away from them. Thus in genuine repentance, man faces judgment, is forgiven, and then sets out on the path of life.

Redemptive repentance demands the response of the whole person. The rational, emotional, and volitional powers unite in the spiritual reconstruction of the personality.

The mind comprehends the inner spiritual disorder. It recognizes the state of estrangement from God. It perceives the human lust for sensate and sinful things. It knows of the stubbornness of the human heart. Psychotherapy emphasizes that there must be knowledge of oneself if one is to be helped. "To know himself as he really is — this is the precondition of all cure, and growth and maturation."[4]

The emotions experience regret and sorrow for personal sin in redemptive repentance. The penitent *feels* like a sinner. His feelings bear witness against all Bushnell-like theories of the innate goodness of man. He feels that the theories do not apply to him. He senses that his own efforts and those of his parents did not bring forth the natural flowering of virtues that some theorists predicted.

The volitional powers determine that a turn in life direction shall be made. If this is not done, then the rational

---

[4]Albert C. Outler, *op. cit.*, p. 170

comprehension of the sinner's situation was only academic and his emotions were a futile exercise in regret and remorse. The action of the will is crucial and decisive. There are dynamic systems of motivation in every life that seek to maintain the present spiritual situation. Habits, as a momentum from the past, tend to keep one going in the old direction of life. The sentiments cling to their objects of attachment. Mental dispositions are persistent in continuing to coerce one to behave as he has behaved before. The combined forces of unregenerated personality make up a heavy spiritual drag. They offer strong resistance to the person seeking a change of life direction. Only decisive volitional action by the grace of God, backed up by the rational and emotional powers, can assure a change of direction.

Redemptive repentance is not morbid. It has all of the anticipation that members of a family have when they examine the old furniture of their home in planning for new equipment. It is like that with a person on the spiritual quest. He examines the old psychological and spiritual furnishings — the attitudes, sentiments, ideals, and habits — and, in the hope of the Gospel, he looks forward eagerly to new spiritual capacities. The anticipation of the new life is motivating. As with Christian in *Pilgrim's Progress*, it causes one to pursue eternal life with decision and persistence.

Man has a yearning for God, a nostalgia for spiritual reality. He has something akin to a homing sense that urges him to turn to God. The Psalmist expressed this sense of longing when he said, "As the hart panteth after the water brooks, so panteth my soul after thee, O God" (Psalm 42:1). Augustine expressed the same idea in his immortal words: "Thou has made us for thyself and our hearts are restless until they rest in thee."[5]

Carl G. Jung, internationally known psychotherapist, believes that the human need for confession and repentance

[5]Augustine, *Confessions* (New York: Liveright Publishing Co.), p. 1.

is written into the very nature of things. He says that it is only by the help of repentance that a man can throw himself "into the arms of humanity, at last freed from the burden of moral exile." If a man does not do this, "an impenetrable wall shuts him from the living experience of feeling himself a man among men."[6] Jung believes that this need for genuine confession is universal. "There appears to be a conscience in mankind which severely punishes the man who does not somehow at sometime, at whatever cost to his pride, cease to assert and defend himself, and instead confess himself fallible and human."[7]

The Hebrew Psalmist, anticipating psychosomatic medicine, said that the need for repentance was inherent in the physical constitution of man. Speaking from personal experience, he said that he suffered ill health when he refused to confess his sin to God.

> When I declared not my sin,
>   my body wasted away
>   through my groaning all day long.
> For day and night thy hand
>   was heavy upon me;
>   my strength was dried up
>   as by the heat of summer
>   (Psalm 32:3,4, R.S.V.)

[6]Carl G. Jung, *Modern Man in Search of a Soul* (London: K. Paul, Trench, Trubner & Co., Ltd., 1933), p. 39.
[7]*Ibid.*

CHAPTER II

Knowing God's Creative Power

God's creative activity continues to be expressed. The Almighty did not stop His creative interest after He spoke the world into existence, but He has maintained this interest to this hour. We can observe clearly His creative power expressed in the lives of men. He brings spiritual order out of the sinful chaos of human hearts. He brings forth new life in the hearts of men whose lives are without spiritual form.

God continues His creative activity in the world of men because it is His very nature to create. It is as difficult to think of God discontinuing His creativity, in the face of human need, as it is to think of a resourceful young man retiring after an initial success. Or, to put it otherwise, a creative and enterprising manufacturer does not abandon all interest in a new factory that he planned and built, feeling that his work was done with the construction of the building. Rather, his creativity continues in the improvement of the methods of production, of the product, and of the equipment.

The central message of the Bible is that divine creativity continues in the hearts of men. Jesus told Nicodemus that spiritual renewal by the power of God was an essential for admittance into the kingdom of God (John 3:5-7). All citizens of that kingdom must experience divine creativity. Paul stated that every man in Christ is "a new creation"

24

(II Corinthians 5:17, r.s.v). Every Christian, says the apostle, is "a new man, which after God is created in righteousness and true holiness" (Ephesians 4:24). Paul sometimes referred to the creative renewal as a spiritual resurrection. "And you he made alive, when you were dead through the trespasses and sins in which you once walked" (Ephesians 2:1, 2a, r.s.v.).

There are numerous analogies of God's creative power in the human heart. God's activity in the spiritual renewal of men, for instance, may be compared to the activity of a radio station that fills a large area of the world with radio waves. This room in which I am writing, for instance, is filled with powerful radio waves. I do not sense them, however, and presumably they are not affecting me. A radio sits on a nearby table, but it is quiet and "lifeless." At this moment I turn on the radio and tune it to a station. The radio is "transformed" and the room is flooded with beautiful music.[1]

Perhaps it is something like that with God's creative activity. He is extending redemptive power toward every person. As long as the sinner remains unyielding to God, like the untuned radio, his life remains unchanged and spiritually lifeless, but when he opens his life to God, divine creative power transforms him.

God's redemptive power, however, is not impersonal, like radio waves. The Old Testament vividly portrays God as looking for men whose hearts are open to Him. "For the eyes of the Lord run to and fro throughout the whole earth, to shew himself strong in the behalf of them whose heart is perfect toward him" (II Chronicles 16:9a). Jesus' earthly ministry was characterized by His search for people whose lives were open to the power of God. "For the son of man is come to seek and to save that which was lost" (Luke 19:10).

[1]Adapted from an illustration given by Dr. Akbar Abdul-Haqq in an address at Asbury Theological Seminary, November 20, 1959.

THE CREATIVE POWER OF DIVINE FORGIVENESS

The forgiveness of sins is a creative act. God brings forth new life through divine forgiveness. He sets free latent human capacities that had long been incapacitated by a frustrating sense of guilt. He redirects energies that had been guilt-ridden and they become constructive. Guilt feelings are disabling; the release of them is life-giving. The significance of God's creativity through forgiveness is seen in viewing the destructive power of a persistent sense of guilt.

Psychiatrists recognize that guilt feelings are debilitating. Neurotic behavior, representing human ineffectiveness and frustration, often results from a sense of guilt. The psychiatrist, William Stekel, says that "every neurotic suffers from a bad conscience." O. H. Mowrer, a psychologist, takes a similar viewpoint. "The neurotic is, without exception in the author's experience, a person who has done things of which he is ashamed, but who, instead of avowing and forsaking his immaturities, has tried instead to deny, repudiate, and repress his own self-condemnation, shame, and guilt."[2] Neuroticism is destructive; adjustment is creative.

Guilt feelings constitute a heavy burden, an intolerable spiritual drag on life. The Hebrew Psalmist expressed this truth in highly picturesque language.

> For my iniquities have
> gone over my head;
> they weigh like a burden too
> heavy for me.
> (Psalm 38:4, R.S.V.)

John Bunyan, with a genius for spiritual perception, shows Christian as bent over physically with his burden of sin as he fled the city of destruction. After his load of sins rolled into the open sepulchre, Christian felt freed and released,

[2]Hobart Mowrer, *Learning Theory and Personality Dynamics* (New York: Ronald, 1950), p. 601.

delivered from the dead weight of the past. His experience represents the feelings of new converts today. They frequently say, "I feel so different," "I feel free."

Guilt feelings are debilitating because they cause one to look backward instead of forward. In doing this, they obscure objectives with a loss of motivation. They consume attention on the wrongs of the past when one ought to be devoted to the urgent demands of the present. Psychic energy is wasted also in the repression of guilt feelings when it ought to be used creatively. A pronounced sense of guilt motivates a fruitless striving for ideals in "a guilt-ridden piety." The endeavor is compulsive, arising as compensatory efforts out of a guilty conscience. The striving is unrewarding and exhausting, lacking both spontaneity and enthusiasm.

Furthermore, guilt feelings are spiritually disabling because they produce anxiety. Anxiety is a psychic and spiritual crippler, as paralysis is to the body. It destroys initiative through a morbid fear of failure. It brings a frustrating timidity into life. It wastes energy in a needless "preparation for disaster." Because of the failures of the past, sometimes exaggerated, it looks forward to the future with apprehension and distrust. It makes the little battles of life into major conflicts and it expends energy in fighting phantom foes. The anxious person lives under a debilitating sense of frustration because large areas of his life are incapacitated by fear.

The release of God-given powers and energies in man through divine forgiveness is a highly significant part of spiritual renewal. It is not, however, all of God's creative action in the matter of making "a new man in Christ." God acts still more directly. He brings forth new springs of life in the heart of the penitent believer.

THE CREATION OF NEW SPIRITUAL DYNAMICS

The New Testament teaches that human nature can be changed, in contrast to the viewpoints in much contemporary human sophistry. Paul refers to the death of the old human disposition and the divine creation of a new one. "We know that our old self was crucified with him so that the sinful body might be destroyed, and we might no longer be enslaved to sin" (Romans 6:6, R.S.V.). Paul stated that every Christian is a new creation. "Therefore, if any man is in Christ, he is a new creation; the old has passed away, behold, the new has come" (II Corinthians 5:17, R.S.V.). He told the Colossians that, as Christians, they "have put off the old nature with its practices and have put on the new nature, which is being renewed in knowledge after the image of its creator" (Colossians 3:9b, 10, R.S.V.).

The experience of the convert confirms the fact of God's creative work within him. William James says that throughout the height of the conversion experience the convert "seems to himself a passive spectator or undergoer of an astonishing process performed upon him from above. There is too much evidence of this for any doubt of it to be possible."[3]

After the conversion experience the convert feels that a miracle has been performed in his heart. James further says:

> It is natural that those who personally have traversed such an experience should carry away a feeling of its being a miracle rather than a natural process. . . . Moreover, the sense of renovation, safety, cleanness, rightness, can be so marvelous and jubilant as well as to warrant one's belief in a radically new substantial nature.[4]

God's creative activity in the hearts of men is not subject to complete human analysis. The process cannot be observed

[3]William James, *Varieties of Religious Experience* (New York: Modern Library, 1902), p. 222.
[4]*Ibid.*, p. 224.

in a laboratory. There is a mystery in it as there are mysteries in other parts of God's creation. The mysteries in the new birth, however, do not forbid one to seek to explain Christian conversion as far as possible in terms of our present understanding of human experience. Such an effort does not minimize the fact of divine creativity; it simply seeks to help make intelligible what God has wrought in the human heart. In other words, it permits a discussion of the new birth in a psychological frame of reference.

The genius of the new birth is seen in the renewal of the basic tendencies of life. Inner dynamics are changed. The driving forces of life are transformed. The systems of motivation are renewed by the Spirit of God. Divine creativity is expressed in the sentiments, attitudes, and interests of life. These are some of the important dynamic systems in human personality.

1. *God transforms sentiments in the new birth.* Sentiments are organized systems of emotionalized tendencies in reference to objects, ideas, and persons. They are the deep personal attachments of people. Sentiments have both rational and emotional elements. They have been called "intellectualized emotions." They are likewise "emotionalized thoughts." Sentiments are driving forces in human personality.

> A sentiment is no mere static fitting of the mind, a simple store house for a cluster of related ideas and values. It is rather a main spring of the individual's life from which radiate all manner of intentions whose purpose is to fulfill the values comprising the sentiment.[5]

Allport says again, "Well-formed, the mature religious sentiment develops a driving power in its own right, motivating action, transforming character, and ordering subjective systems of belief and conduct."[6]

[5]Gordon Allport, *The Individual and His Religion* (New York: Macmillan, 1950), p. 126.
[6]*Ibid.*, p. 109.

Transformed sentiments are basic to Christian living. They provide a frame of reference in which the things of the environment are interpreted. "They act as a comprehensive center of orientation. Most happenings in the environment are seen in relation to them."[7] They give birth to new ideas, saturating each with their own spirit. They originate new purposes and endow them with their own genius. They are the basis for likes and dislikes. They create new habits to implement the purposes of life. They project themselves into the future by creating ideals. They provide an enthusiasm for living.

Transformed sentiments are dynamic in life because they are integrative. Representing the "expulsive power of a new affection," they cast out the old and antithetical loves. Like a great magnet they gather the like elements around them and repel the unlike. A radical change in life depends upon a radical change of sentiments.

> It is simply impossible for the "divided self" — the man torn between conflicting loves — to bring unity into his life by merely saying, "Go to, now. I choose this set of purposes and give up the others." Long continued determination of this sort must indeed have its effect, but before the man can will one set of ends in preference to the other he must have already come to love them best.[8]

2. *God transforms attitudes in the new birth.* The transformation of attitudes gives the Christian life a fine spontaneous quality. The Christian lives in a state of readiness to obey Christ. He has a mental posture to do the will of God.

Attitudes, more specifically, are the spontaneous tendencies to action. They are enduring and learned predisposi-

[7]Solomon E. Asch, *Social Psychology* (New York: Prentice-Hall, 1952), pp. 569-570.
[8]J. B. Pratt, *The Religious Consciousness* (New York: Macmillan, 1920), p. 124.

tions to behave in certain ways toward persons, objects, and ideas. They are less complex than sentiments.

We express our attitudes every day. One has an attitude of economizing in making purchases, so he buys carefully. He has an attitude of kindness to children, and he treats them with great consideration. He has an attitude of respect for all men, so he treats everyone, even the socially disenfranchized, with courtesy and equality. He has an attitude of reverence to God, and he obeys and worships Him.

The New Testament makes clear that the creative power of God changes men's attitudes. Zaccheus, a grasping publican, changed his attitude toward money upon meeting Christ. He stood before the Master and said: "Behold, Lord, the half of my goods I give to the poor; and if I have defrauded any one of anything, I restore it four fold" (Luke 19:8, R.S.V.). Mary Magdalene changed her attitude toward life. She turned from the sordid to the holy. Saul of Tarsus changed his attitude toward Christ and the Christians. He sought out and associated with those whom he had persecuted, and he enthusiastically preached the Gospel he had tried to destroy. Paul told the Ephesians that, upon becoming Christians, they had been delivered from lustful attitudes. They had once lived in the passions of the flesh, following the desires of the body and mind, and so "were by nature children of wrath, like the rest of mankind" (Ephesians 2:3, R.S.V.). By God's grace they had become "his workmanship, created in Christ Jesus for good works" (Ephesians 2:10, R.S.V.).

Starbuck gives numerous testimonies from converted people that illustrate a remarkable change of attitudes. One convert said, "I had more tender feelings for my family and my friends." Another started to reconstruct social relationships on the basis of his new attitudes. "I spoke at once to a person with whom I had been angry." Another said, "I felt for everyone and loved my friends better." Still another spoke of a new attitude of mutuality, "I felt everyone to be my friend." There was also a new attitude of helpfulness in the words of another, "I began to work for others."[9]

3. *God transforms interests in the new birth.* The newly created sentiments become integrative centers for new interests. In this reorganization, some of the old interests are eliminated, others are de-emphasized, and still others, heretofore recessive, become dominant. With spiritual renewal there comes a new internal selectivity of interests and values. The convert is open to, ready for, and warm to some interests. He has a spiritual alertness to them and upon discovering them, he invites them into his life with cordiality. On the other hand, he is callous, cold, and blind to the cheap and sinful things. He has a disposition not to notice them.

A convert, on a flight to Chicago, overheard two conversations. Two men across the aisle talked of their favorite night clubs in Chicago. The convert, having lost all interest in such, was little aware of their conversation. A little later, two men in the seat ahead of his talked of a great evangelistic crusade then in progress in Chicago. The convert was immediately "alive" and responsive as he heard parts of the conversation.

The quality of life depends heavily on the quality of interests. The things to which one gives attention are built into life, like brick and mortar in a building. To change the figure, interests exert a directing force in life by influencing the choice of goals and objectives. They help sustain the sentiments, for better or for worse. They give origin to the formation of habits. "For as he thinketh in his heart, so is he" (Proverbs 23:7a).

Divine creativity in the spiritual renewal of sentiments, attitudes, interests, and every other system of inner dynamics, is the result of divine-human cooperation. God takes

[9]Edwin D. Starbuck, *Psychology of Religion* (New York: Scribner's, n.d.), p. 127.

the initiative and when man responds, the human heart is transformed by divine power. Human effort alone for spiritual renewal is futile. Man cannot save himself. The human response, however, is necessary. Divine power does not work at random in the hearts of men. It is effective only in lives that are open to Him in a living faith.

CHAPTER III

Moving Toward Maturity

God created man with a drive for personal fulfillment. He endowed him with a strong urge to develop his potential worth. Kurt Goldstein, an eminent neuropsychiatrist, believes that the drive for "self actualization" is the most basic motivation in man.[1] Alfred Adler, founder of individual psychology, believes that "the striving for perfection is innate in the sense that it is a part of life, a striving, or an urge, a something without which life would be unthinkable."[2]

Another distinguished psychologist, A. H. Maslow, sees in man a deep tendency "to become actualized in what he is potentially. This tendency might be phrased as a desire to become more and more what one is, to become everything that one is capable of becoming."[3] Man feels that he *must* be what he *can* be. The personally endowed musician must make music, the gifted artist must paint, and the "natural-born" poet must write. A man is not at peace with his inner self if he does not fulfill his inner potentiality, at least to some significant extent.

A crippling sense of disillusionment comes to the man who loses sight of his personal possibilities. Life then takes on a

[1]Kurt Goldstein, *The Organism: A Holistic Approach to Biology Derived from Pathological Data in Man* (New York: American Book Co., 1939), p. 196.

[2]Ansbacher, Heinz L., and Ansbacher, Rowena R., *The Individual Psychology of Alfred Adler* (New York: Basic Books, 1956), p. 104.

[3]A. H. Maslow, *Motivation and Personality* (New York: Harpers, 1954), pp. 91, 92.

debilitating flatness. Speaking for a disillusioned aestheticist, Kierkegaard says, "My soul has lost its (sense of) potentiality. If I were to wish for anything, I should not wish for wealth and power, but for the passionate sense of the potential, for the eye, which ever young and ardent, sees the possible. Pleasure disappoints, possibility never."[4]

The inner urge for self-actualization is expressed in the religious life. The Christian has a deep desire for spiritual wholeness. He, as a child of God, has a profound urge for Christian maturity as surely as a normal boy or girl has an urge for adulthood. Conversion introduces the believer to the spiritual opportunities and strengthens the questing spirit within him. The convert is like a young man who has completed his first semester of study in a graduate school. He sees great possibilities ahead and he is filled with enthusiasm because of the opportunities that await him.

Human life seems to offer only two alternatives in this matter, personal fulfillment or disillusionment; personal attainment or loss of hope. There seems to be a law of nature that a man will be unhappy in the proportion to which he lives below his highest possibilities. This is demonstrated in the lives of thousands of workers in industry who are laboring at jobs far below their mental capacities. It is manifest in the boredom of bright pupils in school who are kept back at the treadmill pace of the average child. It is seen in the lives of Christians who are living far below their spiritual knowledge. One never feels good about an activity to which he has devoted only half interest. Spiritual fixation, like psychological fixation, brings about a sense of personal futility through arrested growth. Every Christian must move toward maturity or suffer from a disabling sense of spiritual frustration.

Forward movement is a law of the spiritual life. One cannot find a stopping place on a spiritual plateau and re-

[4]Soren Kierkegaard, *Either — Or* (Princeton: Princeton University Press, 1944), Vol. I, p. 33.

main there in a state of happy complacency. C. S. Lewis has said pointedly that one cannot go on forever being "a good egg." Sooner or later he will have to turn bad — or hatch.

HUMAN COMMITMENT

A full commitment to Christ is an essential condition for growth toward spiritual maturity. Mature Christian values are not attained on the basis of halfhearted interests. Jesus called for complete devotion to Himself because He knew that the human personality had been created to have only one supreme loyalty. "No man can serve two masters: for either he will hate the one, and love the other; or else he will hold to the one, and despise the other. Ye cannot serve God and mammon" (Matthew 6:24).

The value of commitment to a single purpose is seen in many aspects of life. Commitment enlists all the dynamics of the personality in an effort to achieve a desired objective. It awakens dormant interests. It challenges lethargic talents. It enlists the energies and organizes them in effective effort. It rallies the scattered forces of personality and unites them in a drive to accomplish that which is of supreme personal importance. It concentrates faith on a system of integrated concerns and thus does away with a useless dissipation of energy.

The commitment that fosters growth toward maturity must be more than "an affirmative maybe." It must be a commitment to make God all in all and not an *addition* to the primary interests of life. Spiritual cleansing does not come on the basis of qualified commitments. Jesus did not accept would-be disciples who said, "Lord, I will follow thee *but . . .*" (Luke 9:57-62). They offered no promise of spiritual growth.

Commitment for God's fullness must be more than a "yes — but." Such attitudes lead no place. Alfred Adler used to demonstrate the "yes — but" attitude to his classes by taking one step forward for "yes" and one step backward for "but," with the result that he stood where he was at the beginning.

"A student once remarked, 'I will give God and religion a three-months' trial; if nothing happens, I quit.' He was told that he had quit before he started. God gives no encouragement to experimenters, but he goes a second mile to meet seekers. Seekers are in earnest; experimenters are not."[5] Spiritual maturity is not attained by the religiously tentative. It does not come to those who wish to make short-time commitments with the privilege of canceling or renewing their covenant with God, as a yearly lease on rental property. It is not reached by the spiritually expedient, by those who would make a bargain with God so as to obtain some quick advantages from divine grace.

The nature of God demands full human commitment to Him. "God is either God of all or He is not God at all."[6] It is His very nature to occupy all of life. "What I mean by God," says Melvin E. Wheatley, "is not the manager of a small, fourth-floor department of life called religion. What I mean by God is the owner and operator of the whole business."[7] Halfhearted commitments deprive one of the divinely given spiritual resources. In such a case, one seeks Christian maturity on the basis of human resources, and thus spiritual fulfillment never appears.

There is a type of cleansing power in full commitment. "Purity of heart," says Kierkegaard, "is to will one thing." Thomas Chalmer's classic sermon has contemporary relevance. There is an "expulsive power in a new affection." Complete dedication of life to God eliminates unworthy goals and values from the Christian's psychological field. Christian commitment, as a master sentiment, excludes all that cannot be related to it. It is like a magnet that moves

[5]*Interpreters' Bible* (Nashville: Abingdon-Cokesbury, 1955), Vol. IV, p. 149.
[6]Melvin E. Wheatley in address to National Council of Methodist Youth, *Christian Advocate* (Nov. 26, 1959), p. 6.
[7]*Ibid.*

over a table of miscellaneous particles. It draws the steel filings into its magnetic field but it leaves out the non-metallic substances. The cheap and sinful interests are excluded from the spiritual field of the committed Christian.

Human commitment to worthy purposes has a psychic power to cleanse. One observes the cleansing power of commitment in nonreligious areas of life. A young man in his late teens is captured by a challenging life profession. He wishes to become a doctor. Commitment to that purpose eliminates some of his former interests. He has little concern, for instance, in spending his evenings at the soda fountain of a corner drug store and engaging in adolescent banter.

There is a more profound type of cleansing than the psychic cleansing that is realized by a commitment to a person or a purpose. This is divine cleansing. It is a type of spiritual cleansing in depth that comes about through the power of the Holy Spirit as a Christian commits his life fully to God. This kind of commitment represents an opening of the life to the Spirit of God. It is an entrustment of the life to God. In response to the believer's commitment and faith the Holy Spirit cleanses the desires and affections of the devoted Christian.

DIVINE CLEANSING

Spiritual cleansing is a basic condition in the attainment of spiritual maturity. Spiritual cleansing sometimes is called simply sanctification which may be defined as "the action of the Holy Spirit in making holy the believer by imparting in him the Christian graces and the destruction of the sinful affections."[8]

The Acts of the Apostles portrays vividly that the presence of God, through the fullness of the Holy Spirit, brings spiritual cleansing. The disciples were filled with the Holy Spirit

[8]James A. H. Murray, A *New English Dictionary on Historical Principles* (Oxford: Clarendon Press, 1901), Vol. VIII, Part II, p. 80.

on the day of Pentecost and their hearts were purified. After twenty years of personal experience and perspective following Pentecost, Peter said, "And God, which knoweth the hearts, bare them witness (Cornelius and the members of his household), giving them the Holy Ghost, even as he did unto us (on the day of Pentecost); and put no difference between us and them, purifying their hearts by faith" (Acts 15:8, 9). Peter spoke these words at the Council of Jerusalem which had been called to define certain Christian positions. The seasoned apostle, sensing the importance of the meeting, spoke in precise and exact terms about basic matters. A study of the attitudes of the disciples validates Peter's statement about the significance of Pentecost to them.

Before Pentecost Peter himself was filled with strange and contradictory attitudes. There were times when he was self-sacrificing, but at other times he was self-seeking (Mark 1:18; Matthew 19:27). He was gifted with spiritual insight yet on occasion he was slow to grasp the deeper truths (John 6:68; Matthew 15:15, 16). He made two great confessions of his faith in Christ but he also made a strong denial (Matthew 16:16; John 6:69; Mark 14:67-71). He demonstrated a reckless courage in attacking a servant of the high priest in the Garden of Gethsemane, but a few hours later he, in a cowardly way, denied any knowledge of Jesus (Matthew 26:51, 69-74).

James and John, as reputable representatives of the disciples before Pentecost, also demonstrated spiritual ambivalence. They were go-getters, personally ambitious to advance above their fellows even if this had to be done through a conniving mother seeking preferences for them (Matthew 20:20-28). They were rash in their assertions that they were qualified to occupy chief seats in a spiritual kingdom, not knowing that they had the spirit of the world (Matthew 20:22). Moreover, they were vindictive. They stood outside an inhospitable Samaritan village one evening with Jesus and the other disciples and wished to call down fire from heaven to destroy the hapless inhabitants (Luke 9:51-56). Some of the early ancient texts of this account state, as does the King James Version, that they gave their vindictive request a note of sanctity by referring to the fact that Elijah had used that method of handling difficult situations. Jesus rebuked them for their spirit. He knew that they were not yet ready to build a spiritual kingdom if they could not accept with poise the slights and discourtesies of the world.

Thomas, the doubter, gave little prospect of spiritual effectiveness before Pentecost. He was hesitant and unbelieving. The most prominent thing about him seems to be his lack of faith. The gospel records give more attention to this than to any other aspect of his personality. One of the last glimpses we get of him before Pentecost tells about his arbitrary declaration that he would not believe in the risen Christ "Except I shall see in his hands the print of the nails, and put my finger into the print of the nails, and thrust my hand into his side" (John 20:25). How could Jesus use such a positivist to advance a spiritual kingdom? What could a doubter like Thomas accomplish in a movement based on faith? He would always raise two questions for every single affirmation.

All the disciples were earthly minded before Pentecost. They viewed the kingdom of God as an earthly kingdom. In their last conversation with Jesus, as they walked with Him to Mt. Olivet before His ascension, they kept asking Him if He would not restore the kingdom to Israel (Acts 1:6). The verb translated "asked" in Acts 1:6 is in the imperfect tense in the Greek text and it suggests that they repeatedly asked Him that question before He answered. This shows their great concern about earthly things. They were still unprepared to build a spiritual kingdom while thoughts of earthly grandeur were uppermost in their minds.

The apostles displayed a new quality of life immediately after Pentecost. Peter proclaimed the resurrection of Jesus with courage and power, publicly charging the leaders of the Jews with putting the Messiah to death (Acts 2:23). The other disciples were Peter's assistants. They too proclaimed Christ's death and the Resurrection. Peter did not seem to be the same man that he had been fifty days before at which time he stood before a curious damsel and denied having had any association with Jesus. The other disciples did not seem like the same men who fled from Jesus in fear on the night of the betrayal.

The cleansing power of the Holy Spirit extended into other areas of the disciples' lives. The old vindictive spirit was gone and they suffered persecution in love. There is no record of their clamoring for chief seats. They had a nonchalance about earthly kingdoms and wealth and they established a plan of generous sharing so that human need could be met (Acts 2:45). They were filled with a passion for preaching and they went everywhere proclaiming the Gospel. Tradition says that the one-time doubter, Thomas, went all the way to India and established Christianity there. James preached so plainly that he met an early martyrdom. Perhaps the others joined him in death in like manner, excepting John, the one-time son of thunder, who became an apostle of love.[9]

There is a splendid spiritual simplicity about spiritual cleansing. God's presence, typified by fire, cleanses what it fills. His presence made holy the ground about the burning bush in the days of Moses (Exodus 3:2-5). Today, God's fullness in the human heart makes it holy. The Christian receives cleansing when he opens every area of his life to God's fullness. The poet, T. E. Brown, observed that the crucial point here is the human willingness to let the Holy Spirit possess all of life:

[9]While the lives of the apostles were revolutionized indeed on the day of Pentecost, it must be recognized that the Holy Spirit did not immediately resolve all of their old prejudices. Prejudices concerning food and the eating with Gentiles created spiritual problems for Peter (Acts 10:9-16; Galatians 2:11-14).

If thou canst empty all thyself of self,
Like a shell disinhabitated,
Then might he find thee on the ocean shelf,
And say — "This is not dead" —
And fill thee with himself instead.

But thou art all replete with very *thou*,
And hast such shrewd activity,
That when he comes he says — This is enow
Unto itself — 'Twere better let it be:
It is so small and full, there is no room for me.[10]

When the Holy Spirit possesses fully a human life He "scatters his life through every part, and sanctifies the whole." He shares His nature, characterized by holiness, embodied in His very name, with the believer who has committed his all to Him. The believer is made a partaker of the divine nature through the sanctifying power of the Spirit of God (II Peter 1:4). As natural life is the product of divine power alone, so the spiritual life is the result of the indwelling Spirit in the heart of the believer.

Paul presents a most convincing and graphic statement of spiritual cleansing in the seventh and eighth chapters of his epistle to the Romans. He describes the inner struggle between human nature and a sense of righteousness in the seventh chapter. He portrays vividly the victory of righteousness over the lower human nature in the eighth chapter. These chapters should always be read together. To read the seventh chapter as a unit in itself is like reading the earlier part of a climactic battle in a history book and putting the book aside without reading the outcome.

In his portrayal of spiritual victory over sin in human nature, Paul states that the law, as set forth in the Old Testament, never succeeded in producing righteousness because of the weakness of human nature (Romans 8:3). "But God met this by sending His only son Jesus Christ to live

[10]T. E. Brown, "Indwelling," *The Collected Poems of T. E. Brown* (London: Macmillan, 1900), pp. 82, 83.

in the human nature that causes the trouble" (Romans 8:3, as translated by J. B. Phillips in *Letters to Young Churches*). Paul restates this revolutionary truth several times in the eighth chapter of Romans. "But ye are not carnal but spiritual if the Spirit of God finds a home within you" (Romans 8:9, in Phillips, *op. cit.*). He re-emphasizes it by equating the indwelling Christ with the Holy Spirit. "Now if Christ does live within you His presence means that your sinful nature is dead, but your spirit becomes alive because of the righteousness He brings with Him" (Romans 8:10, Phillips, *op. cit.*).

The permanence of spiritual cleansing is seen in the continuing and the dynamic relationship between the Holy Spirit and the believer. As with the apostles on the day of Pentecost, Christian cleansing is effected at the moment of the believer's full commitment of self to God by faith in Christ. In one sense, then, cleansing represents a state of grace. It is not static, however. It is not a spiritual estate to which one receives a life lease. Spiritual cleansing, as a condition for maturity, is maintained by a dynamic sense of commitment and by a living faith in Christ. The moment by moment relationship with Christ is even more important than its beginning. The happily married couple, for instance, does not overly emphasize their wedding day. The wedding ceremony did indeed bring them into a state of marriage, but their love matures as they maintain mutual interests, constant loyalty, and high ideals.

CHAPTER IV

Living With Confidence

E. Stanley Jones says, "Those of us who have been up against raw human need for years know that men need nothing, absolutely nothing, so much as they need the simple assurance that they are reconciled to God. Unhealed at that place, men wear a mortal hurt."[1] Jones speaks out of years of missionary experience. He has observed often the human cry for personal religious certitude.

Furthermore, this veteran missionary considers the sense of divine acceptance as the climaxing life experience. "The assurance that the grace of God in Christ banishes estrangement and reconciles to God is the most precious thing that ever sunk into guilty human hearts."[2]

Theologians and some psychotherapists agree that a lack of a sense of God's acceptance often causes serious spiritual and psychological problems. This lack, interpreted as personal rejection, becomes the seedbed for a debilitating sense of inferiority, morbid guilt feelings, anxiety, and hostility. All of these demand a heavy toll of life. The toll runs all the way from a slackening in "the onward march of life" to complete incapacity.

A part of the genius of the Christian faith is seen in the sense of certainty that Christ gives to His followers. They have confidence that they are in a right relationship with God. Many of the early Christians demonstrated this clearly.

[1]E. Stanley Jones, *Victorious Living* (New York: Abingdon, 1936), p. 59.
[2]*Ibid.*

They spoke of their spiritual relationships with an amazing confidence. "And by this we may be sure that we know him, if we keep his commandments" (I John 2:3, R.S.V.). The divine presence was so real in their hearts that they said with a steadfast conviction, "By this we know that we abide in him and he in us, because he has given us of his Spirit" (I John 4:13, R.S.V.). They talked of their spiritual transformation with astonishing assurance. "We know that we have passed out of death into life, because we love the brethren" (I John 3:14).

Following Paul's day the early Christians were able to "outlive the world" because they had a sense of divine acceptance. Recognizing themselves as members of "a third race," as citizens of heaven, they demonstrated a superlative quality of life in a decadent age. They had personal surety in a time of doubt. They had a sense of direction in an age of aimlessness. They had luminous personal objectives when men about them saw nothing for which to live. They had compelling interests in a time when life had gone flat to others. They had a sense of abiding values in an age of disillusionment. They envisioned "the city of God" when it appeared that the world was falling apart.

THE CONTENT OF CHRISTIAN ASSURANCE

It is hard to define adequately the essence of the experience of Christian assurance. John Wesley, modern recoverer of this doctrine of assurance, said that it was difficult to find words in the language of men to explain "the deep things of God." The difficulty lies in "trying to think nonsensuous objects in a sensuous way." It is hard indeed to express spiritual ideas in the vocabulary of a sensate and materialistic age. Moreover, in any generation, actual life goes beyond words. Every man ought to live beyond his vocabulary. This, too, makes it hard to define the living content of the doctrine of Christian assurance. In spite of the difficulties, however, we shall look at Christian assurance and seek to state a part of its meaning in words. Having done this, we shall leave the undefined residue to be realized in the life of the sincere believer.

Christian assurance is personal certitude, a feeling of certainty, of one's own salvation. It is an "intuitive certitude" of a filial relationship with God. It is a confidence that one is in a right relationship with Jesus Christ through a living faith in Him. The concept is exceptionally rich in its spiritual overtones. "It signifies the joyous, unwavering confidence of an intelligent faith; the security of a fearless trust."[3]

Christian assurance is a divine-human outcome. God and man work together in bringing it about. It has divinely given and humanly achieved elements. Both are essential and it is necessary to view each of them clearly if Christian assurance is to be understood. Christian certitude appears highly mystical and unreal if one looks only at the divine element. It seems superficial and unstable if one looks only at its human aspects.

The Divine Element. God provides a basis for Christian assurance in the twofold work of grace that He accomplishes in the heart of the believer. To be more specific, Christian assurance is related integrally to both personal justification and to spiritual regeneration. Divine forgiveness, as the essence of justification, suggests divine acceptance. The convert knows that it was his sins that had separated him from God. With their forgiveness, he feels that he is restored to his relationship to God. Secondly, the new life realized in personal regeneration suggests divine approval. The convert believes that the new birth is given only to those whom God accepts.

Moreover, in addition to God's twofold work in the heart of the convert, the abiding presence of the Holy Spirit in the believer's life provides a basis for Christian confidence. There are many meaningful deductions from the Spirit's

[3]Dwight M. Pratt, "Assurance," *The International Standard Encyclopedia* (Chicago: Howard-Severance Co., 1915), Vol. I, p. 290.

presence. His guidance suggests unity of purpose between Himself and the believer. His revelation of divine truth suggests mutual trust. The Spirit's empowerment points to His confidence in the believer's sincerity. His helpfulness shows the divine-human cooperation in the achievement of spiritual purposes. This divine-human association and cooperation provide a strong basis for a sense of divine acceptance. It points to the fact that the Holy Spirit, who is never casual in His workings, has chosen the believer as one through whom He can reveal Himself.

Finally, Paul teaches that the Holy Spirit takes a still more direct action in assuring the believer of his salvation. He gives the believer a "sense of belonging." In his classic statement in Romans 8:15, 16, R.S.V., Paul says, "For you did not receive the spirit of slavery to fall back into fear, but you have received the spirit of sonship. When we cry, 'Abba! Father!' it is the Spirit himself bearing witness with our spirit that we are the children of God. . . ." His statement in Galatians 4:6, R.S.V., is equally graphic. "And because you are sons, God has sent the Spirit of his Son into our hearts crying, 'Abba! Father!' "

Paul refers to the strength of the assurance that comes from the Holy Spirit. To emphasize this thought he uses the Greek word *kradzon* which means "to cry, to shriek." These were certainly not audible cries. Paul was referring to a type of communication that brings the same kind of certitude that strongly spoken words bring about.

The genius of the Spirit's communication of assurance is seen in a sense of sonship. The believer *feels* like a son. He has a consciousness that God is his Father and he spontaneously calls Him, "Father," as a child uncritically calls his father, "Father." The Spirit communicates a sense of belonging, a recognition of spiritual relationships, a feeling of at-homeness with spiritual things. He gives a perception of mutual interests. The sense of sonship, as given by the Spirit, is a substantial fact in the Christian life. When confirmed by actual human experience, it becomes the basis for confident living.

The Human Element. The human mind with its marked power for creative insight cooperates with the Spirit in providing a sense of Christian certitude. The mind, as a great synthesizer, looks at the facts of life in relation to spiritual realities and it formulates an insight that has great worth. In doing this, the mind views the attitudes, interests, sentiments, ideals, and habits of life. It looks also into the past and evaluates the decisive moments. It examines the basic motives of past endeavor. It considers the aspiration, yearnings, and motives of the present moment. It looks closely at the emotional side of life. Having done all this, much of it on the unconscious level, the mind then relates all these factors to spiritual reality and reports to the sincere believer that he belongs to God.

This insight, derived from the actual materials of life, bears the mark of authenticity. It seems genuine because it came right out of life. The believer observes the marks of coherence upon it. He recognizes elements that entered its structure. He observes the relationship of the whole to the constituent parts.

The Christian should give careful consideration to all such insights. "The human mind is the most delicate of all recording instruments. . . . (It) is the only agency ever devised for registering at once innumerable variables and for the *revealing relationships between them*"[4] (italics are Allport's). These words, written twenty-five years ago by a distinguished psychologist, before the extensive development of computing machines, express a great truth. With all due respect to IBM, one can predict that the superiority of the human mind for synthesizing the personal facts of life is not threatened by any mechanical computer.

The thoughtful Christian, however, does not accept the

[4]Gordon Allport, *Personality, a Psychological Interpretation* (New York: Henry Holt and Co., 1937), p. 547.

mind's intuitive insight alone as the final human answer relative to personal salvation. He seeks to confirm the insight by a number of deliberate and objective approaches. He looks to memory for the recall of personal repentance and faith in Christ. He remembers the sense of release from sin that came in the moment of forgiveness. He examines his life carefully to make sure that there has been a new and abiding spiritual strength. He looks to his critical faculties to report a positive correspondence between the New Testament principles of Christian living and his actual practice. The practical-minded John Wesley emphasized this point. He believed that the best confirmation of the inner and direct witness of the Spirit was the presence of the fruit of the Spirit in the Christian's life.

CHRISTIAN ASSURANCE AND PSYCHIC NEEDS

Our generation has four basic psychic problems. (1) Modern man feels estranged from God, that is, from His essential Being, and often he senses that he is estranged from his fellow men. (2) He is filled with hostility as shown by personal antagonisms and by the persistence of the cold war and the massive military preparations. (3) He is anxiety-ridden in spite of a great accumulation of wealth and the extensive development of programs of security. Finally, (4) he possesses a sense of futility and feelings of emptiness about life.

The message of Christian assurance has a healing word for each of these problems. The recognition of one's relationship to God, through the grace of Christ, substitutes an attitude of belonging for a sense of estrangement; it dispells hostilities; it removes a basic cause for anxiety; and it gives meaning and zest to life.

1. *The feeling of human estrangement from God is caused largely by a sense of guilt.* Man feels estranged from God, His essential Being, because he has sinned against Him. This is portrayed graphically in the biblical story of Adam

and Eve, an account with enduring psychological-spiritual significance. The first couple, having sinned, *felt* estranged from God before He spoke words of judgment. They demonstrated their sense of estrangement by hiding from Him in the garden. They exhibited the law that is written deeply in human nature, namely, that unforgiven sin causes feelings of estrangement and rejection.

The prophet Isaiah states this principle as universal law. "But your iniquities have separated between you and your God, and your sins have hid his face from you, that he will not hear" (Isaiah 59:2). The Hebrew Psalmist also emphasized that sin separates from God. "If I regard iniquity in my heart, the Lord will not hear me" (Psalm 66:18).

Man is restive with a sense of estrangement. He wishes to be related to both his Creator and to his fellow men. "Psychotherapy has pointed out that man needs nothing so much as relief from the sense of isolation and estrangement."[5] Some psychotherapists believe that this principle applies to God's acceptance as much as to human approval.

A sense of Christian assurance strikes at the very heart of the problem of human estrangement. An attitude of acceptance by God precludes the opposite attitude of estrangement. One cannot have both at the same time. Furthermore, a sense of acceptance with God relates one to his fellow men. As one feels related to the Father he feels also related to His children.

2. *The sense of unforgiven sin is productive of extensive hostility in man.* Human experience shows that people tend to be hostile, consciously or unconsciously, toward those by whom they feel rejected. Feeling rejected by God, man starts setting up his own little competitive world. He elevates himself to the center of it, and prescribes his own laws and practices, in hostile disregard to the divine commandments.

King Saul shows how hostility develops out of a sense

[5]Bonthius, Robert H., *Christian Pathways to Self Assurance* (New York: King's Crown Press, 1948), p. 203.

of divine rejection and estrangement. The personal history of Saul from the time of his rejection shows increasing hostility to God and man. He compulsively pursued David, God's anointed, in a state of neurotic anxiety. His hostility to God was projected onto David, the living symbol of God's rejection of him.

Observation of life about us shows that there is a vast amount of overt and explicit hostility toward God. It is shown by man's arrogant and willful independence from God with the insistence that he alone direct his life. It is seen in many religious people by a substitution of "pious" works while they persistently direct their inner lives as they wish. Hostility toward God is shown by erudite professors in colleges and universities who belittle the Almighty, substituting their tentative hypotheses for His infinite wisdom. The extensive practice of cursing and swearing reveals the large amount of hostility to God. Men blaspheme the name of their Benefactor because they are inwardly hostile to Him. They impiously use His name, casting their profanities toward heaven, as small boys throwing stones at a stranger whom they consider to be unfriendly.

Hostility is one of modern man's greatest problems. Paul Tillich asserts that there is extensive hostility to God even in the hearts of good men. "Have you ever noticed how much hostility against God dwells in the depths of good and honest people, in those who excel in works of charity, in piety and religious zeal?"[6] Who can say that Tillich is wrong here in view of the fact that would-be good people often repress their hostilities?

A sense of Christian assurance does much to do away with the impulse of hostility. Feelings of acceptance displace feelings of rejection. God is viewed as a benefactor instead of as an enemy. The whole disposition is to cooperate with the One to whom he belongs. Attitudes of cooperation displace

[6]Paul Tillich, *The New Being* (New York: Scribners, 1955), p. 20.

attitudes of hostility toward men. John emphasizes that love is pervasive in life (I John 3:18).

3. *The sense of unforgiven sin is productive of anxiety.* The anxious person is jostled about by the ghosts of forgotten sins and repressed failures, both moral and nonmoral. Many psychiatrists believe that repressed guilt feelings form the seedbed of many anxieties. Karen Horney thought that there is a growing conviction among psychiatrists that guilt feelings are basic to personality maladjustments that are characterized by anxiety.[7] William Stekel, a psychiatrist, believed that every neurotic suffers from a bad conscience.

There are many reasons why a sense of unforgiven sin causes anxiety. The sinner is anxious because he feels estranged from and rejected by God because of his impenitent sins. He feels insecure — cut off from His essential Being. He feels anxious because of his hostile attitudes which he inwardly dislikes. He is fearful because of an anticipation of the final judgment. He has "a certain fearful looking for of judgment and fiery indignation" (Hebrews 10:27). Recognizing that he is defenseless before the Almighty, he believes that "it is a fearful thing to fall into the hands of the living God."

The spirit of man demands more than existential security — a good job, an adequate income, and money in the bank. Intuiting its immortality, the spirit wishes security in the beyond. The spiritually sensitive soul becomes anxious when this is lacking. Kierkegaard was thinking along this line when he spoke of the anxiety (or dread) that arises out of the "dizziness of freedom."[8] This dizziness, which is a dizziness of responsibility, comes when one looks down the "yawning abyss" of human possibility and recognizes that he has not made good use of his opportunities.

Christian assurance has an answer for anxiety. The sense

[7]Karen Horney, *The Neurotic Personality of Our Time* (New York: W. W. Norton and Co., 1937), pp. 230-258.

[8]Soren Kierkegaard, *The Concept of Dread* (Princeton: Princeton University Press, 1944), pp. 55-56.

of divine forgiveness allays anxiety through a confidence that there has been a pre-judgment settlement of sin on the basis of mercy instead of wrath. The forgiven man looks forward to his eternal future with anticipation instead of with anxiety; with faith instead of with fear. A sense of gratitude displaces a sense of guilt, and confidence takes the place of condemnation. Paul illustrates this vividly in Romans 8. He starts his thought there with the declaration, "There is therefore now no condemnation to them which are in Christ Jesus" (Romans 8:1a). As he proceeds in his thinking, he gives literature's clearest statement of Christian assurance, "The Spirit itself beareth witness with our spirit, that we are the children of God" (Romans 8:16). He then moves on to his climax in which he gives a vivid expression of his anticipation of the future. He states in the most exalted words that nothing in the present or future shall ever be able to separate us from the love of Christ (Romans 8:35-39).

4. *The sense of divine acceptance gives meaning to life, delivering one from a frustrating sense of futility and emptiness.* This, too, is a basic need of the human race. Man, created in the image of God, is "overbuilt for this world." He is essentially a spiritual being with a spiritual disposition, needs, and capacities. He cannot be satisfied with sensate things only. He longs for "soul-sized" objectives. In moments of quietness, he intuits that many of his interests are too little for his immortal spirit. He wants a longer time perspective than seventy or eighty years of earthly existence. His essential self longs for an "extension of life" that has both qualitative and quantitative dimensions.

A thoughtful view of contemporary life points out an extensive lack of a satisfying sense of purpose. Many in our generation are "suffering from nothingness." Gertrude Stein describes intellectuals whom she met in Paris, "as belonging to nothing, and mastered by no great loyalty. They had 'no gods to serve.'" These people, like Tolstoi before his conversion, found that "life came to a standstill, and turned sinister."[9] They typify a large number today who are like:

> A soldier who is without zeal for fighting,
> A poet without zeal for writing,
> An architect without a plan:
> The prototype of modern man.[10]

T. S. Eliot describes vividly the frustrating situation of people caught in feelings of futility.

> . . . the stained time ridden faces,
> Distracted from distraction by distraction,
> Filled with fancies and empty meaning,
> Tumid apathy with no concentration
> Men and bits of paper, whirled by the cold wind. . . .[11]

Leo Tolstoi gives eloquent witness that things alone cannot satisfy the immortal spirit. Life came to a standstill for him in spite of his wealth and distinction. "I felt that the ground on which I stood was crumbling, that there was nothing for me to stand on, that what I had been living for was nothing, that I had no reason for living. . . ."[12] He found purpose in life through a sense of divine acceptance.

Many in our generation go to psychiatrists to find meaning in life when they should seek it in forgiveness. Carl Jung mentions this class of patients.

> Among my patients from many countries, all of them educated persons, there is a considerable number who came to see me, not because they were suffering from a neurosis, but because they could find no meaning in life or were torturing themselves with questions which neither present-day philosophy nor religion could answer.[13]

[9]Stephan Zweig, *The Living Thoughts of Tolstoi* (New York: Longmans, Green & Co.), p. 3.
[10]John C. Cooper, in *The Christian Century*, Jan. 1, 1958, p. 16.
[11]T. S. Eliot, "Four Quartets," *The Complete Poems and Plays* (New York: Harcourt, Brace and Company, 1952), p. 120.
[12]Stephan Zweig, *op. cit.*, p. 37.
[13]Carl Jung, *Modern Man in Search for a Soul* (New York: Harcourt, Brace & Co., n.d.), pp. 266-267.

Jung further describes some of these patients as bewildered because of the meaninglessness of life.

> How often have I heard a patient exclaim, "If I only knew that my life had some meaning and purpose, then there would be no silly story about my nerves!" Whether the person is rich or poor, has family or social position or not, alters nothing, for outer circumstances are far from giving his life a meaning.[14]

Man, created with the Eternal within him, tires of wading in the shallows of life. He wants to be where it is deeper. He fears, however, to go into the deep because a sensate culture has roped off a little wading place on the beach. He stifles his yen for the beyond by occupying himself with his fellows, like children playing in the shallow water.

When Samuel Wesley was dying he turned to his son, John, and said, "The inward witness — this is the proof, the strongest proof of Christianity."[15] The elder Wesley had made a great discovery in his personal spiritual quest in a day when it was generally thought that the doctrine of Christian assurance was fanatical. Samuel Wesley found the inward witness sufficient in the crisis of death.

The doctrine of Christian assurance is a part of the distinctive glory of the Christian faith. It is a part of God's great therapy for guilt-ridden men. Psychology has no satisfying answer to the guilt problem. "It may bring relief by confession and by release of emotion accompanying it, but it can never bring the peace and assurance of forgiveness."[16] Through Christian assurance, God offers man freedom from the bondage of the past, confident living for the present, and a sure hope for the future.

[14]*Ibid.*, p. 224.
[15]Townsend, William S., Eayrs, and Workman, *A New History of Methodism*, Nashville: Publishing House of Methodist Episcopal Church South, n.d.), Vol. I, p. 168.
[16]Ernest White, *Christian Life and the Unconscious* (New York: Harper and Bros., 1955), p. 156.

Part II
Keeping Spiritually Fit

CHAPTER V

Understanding Maladjustive Impulses

Henri Bergson says that "while we think with only a small part of our past, it is with our entire past . . . that we desire and will and act." The past life of each of us continues to provide motivation. There is a push of the past. Many of the forgotten experiences remain dynamic and they exercise an influence on our present behavior. The constructive experiences of life provide an onward thrust, but the maladjustive experiences constitute a spiritual drag.

Acknowledging the Complexes

A complex is a group of emotionally charged desires, ideas, and attitudes. It may be either conscious or unconscious; either constructive or maladjustive in personality. The unconscious and maladjustive complexes are of particular interest to us in this discussion.

Repressed or unconscious complexes often have their origin in experiences of frustration usually in early life. There are numerous instances of this. The so-called "inferiority complex," for example, arises out of repeated experiences of personal failure or out of attitudes of depreciation from others. Also, the highly authoritarian father, lacking an understanding of his sensitive boy, sometimes brings about an authority complex in his son that motivates him later either to fear or to resent all authority figures in his life. Again, unwholesome information about sex sometimes gives rise to a complex of emotionally toned ideas about that phase of life.

Repressed complexes exert an enormous influence on human behavior. They are some of the deeply moving drives of human personality. They are particularly influential because of the emotional elements in them. They usually remain dynamic after one has discovered their existence. For instance, a man may become aware of his cowardice but that recognition does not make him courageous. He will continue to experience impulses of cowardice until he comes to understand the reasons for his abnormal fear and, perhaps, until he lives through experiences that reduce the emotions of his complex.

Complexes give rise to motivations toward wrongdoing, as well as to other types of maladjustive behavior.[1] They are thus of primary importance in the spiritual life. They provide urges to wrongdoing though they are not sinful themselves. Often they do not arise in situations that are morally evil. Not everything that provides a motivation toward wrong acts is sinful in itself.

This means that there are two interior sources that provide urges to wrong-doing in the human personality. First, there are the natural and inborn tendencies to sin which theologians have termed original or innate sin. Second, there are the repressed complexes and the maladjustive impulses which have been acquired in life experiences. Original sin is seen primarily in an inborn disposition to be at enmity with God (Romans 8:7). It is an innate drive in man to have his own way. It is an inherent impulse for man "to be his own supreme arbiter." The Thirty-nine Articles of Religion of the Church of England define original, or innate sin, as "the fault and corruption of every man, whereby man is very far gone from original righteousness, and is of his own nature inclined to evil, so that the flesh lusteth always con-

[1]The term "motivation" is used here to suggest all the impulses to action, both conscious and unconscious, as well as the deliberate intentions. Many times the deliberate motives are in conflict with urges that arise out of the unconscious.

trary to the spirit. . . ." On the other hand, the repressed complexes and maladjustive impulses are centers of psychic energy that have been built up through frustrating experiences in life. Naturally, these centers of psychic energy are greater in some people than in others depending upon the degree of personality adjustment that they have attained. However, no one presumably is totally free from maladjustive impulses.

To be more specific, original sin, as seen in the carnal nature of man, consists of those tendencies in sinful human nature that are rooted in the flesh or in the human body. Original sin suggests all that is fallen and sinful in human nature. Carnal living suggests living according to the impulses of the flesh. Paul identified the carnal mind with "the law of death." He says that it makes a man be at "enmity against God" (Romans 8:1-8). Carnal desires are rooted in human pride, a sense of self will, a desire for self aggrandizement, and an arrogance toward God.

The tendencies that arise out of repressed experiences are qualitatively different. The goal of these impulses is toward the things that belong to essential self-hood: a sense of personal security, an attitude of acceptance by others, and healthy feelings of self-esteem. Thus, maladjustive impulses seek the normal and right ends of life but they often seek them by wrong means. The person with inferiority feelings wishes to be considered as adequate and capable but, to obtain proper consideration, he is sometimes inwardly tempted to pretend that he is better than he is. The man who feels rejected by others may be tempted from within to get a right measure of acceptance by a compromise of standards. Neither the wish to be considered adequate nor the desire to be accepted is rooted in the sinful nature of man. It is something that God wishes for all of His children.

Wherein then is the evil in maladjustive impulses if they seek ends that rightly belong to human existence? These impulses are unconscious and uncritical. They are not judicious as to means to obtain the right ends that they seek. The impulse from an inferiority complex may go in the direction of depreciating others in search of a sense of adequacy. An impulse from within a person that has lacked a sense of personal freedom may move in the direction of antagonism toward all authority in a search for a healthy sense of autonomy and freedom. These impulses are amoral, rooted in a complex of personal psychological need. They must be directed by the conscious mind. They become personally sinful only when the conscious approves of the use of wrong means.

The difficulty of knowing precisely the spiritual quality of one's impulses does not diminish the value of understanding clearly that there is a difference between emotional complexes and human carnality, though they seem closely intertwined in actual life experiences. In spite of the difficulties, it is important that we recognize the fact that maladjustive psychological processes differ from innate sin. We must see clearly that defense mechanisms and depravity are not the same. One should not think of the maladjustive impulses as "acquired depravity"; they are accumulated and frustrated needs of the personality. Their motivation, however, is much like that of innate sin. Christians come into confusion when they do not recognize that acquired psychic reactions often provide urges to unchristian behavior and that they give rise to a resistance to the will of God.

Many advocates of the deeper spiritual life have invalidated their message by claiming too much. They have failed to discriminate between the innate sinful impulses and the acquired tendencies that originated in unfavorable life experiences. They have overlooked the fact that tendencies to wrongdoing may spring even from a sanctified life. With an attitude of overgeneralization, they have failed to see that emotionally toned ideas become drives to action; that repressed experiences provide motivation in behavior; and that traumatic experiences remain dynamic after they have been forgotten. Many ardent advocates for the deeper spiritual life have forgotten that truth is obscured by overstatement as well as by understatement.[2]

The sincere person on the Christian quest becomes confused and disillusioned when he fails to recognize that the Holy Spirit does not cleanse away, like a great divine psychiatrist, all the emotional complexes, defense mechanisms, anxieties, and other ineffective psychological processes when He fills the human heart with His sanctifying presence.[3] Paul recognized that many of the psychic processes remain in the heart after the filling of the Spirit. After describing personal freedom from the "law of sin and death" in Romans 8, he says, "Likewise the Spirit also helpeth our infirmities" (Romans 8:26a). The Holy Spirit employs a different kind of divine therapy in resolving the acquired tendencies to wrongdoing. He does not remove all of them by an act of cleansing, but rather He helps believers to gain insight into their maladjustments and to resolve them by His strengthening presence.

SEEKING INSIGHT

It is more difficult, unfortunately, to determine the quality of one's urges in actual life than to discuss them in theory. For one thing, we are often hindered in seeing ourselves. Personal prejudices, obsessional thoughts, compulsive patterns of behavior, and emotionally charged ideas obscure

[2]Many of the leaders in the deeper life movements have recognized human frailty in what they call the "human element." This constituted a drag on the spiritual life and sometimes led the believer into deliberate sin. Few of the writers on the deeper Christian life have been sufficiently specific in defining the precise nature of the "human element" in Christian experience. Few have given attention to the repressed emotional factors that remain dynamic in the personality.

[3]It should be recognized that the presence of the Holy Spirit in the human personality does affect the total psychic and spiritual life. The Spirit's abiding fullness often reduces the energy of the maladjustive impulses and sometimes it eliminates them altogether. At other times, and for a variety of reasons, certain complexes and impulses remain after one has had faith for spiritual cleansing. It is with these that we are primarily concerned in this chapter.

our views of the inner self. Thus, our spiritual vision is dull.

Moreover, actual life is more complex than the theories about it, and urges usually are not simply moral or non-moral, spiritual or carnal. A large part of human existence presents motives that have both maladjustive and sinful elements. Man has no spiritual microscope by which he can identify neatly the various elements. This problem, however, must not cause him to become unconcerned about the quality of his urges. The best rule is seen in a rugged personal honesty about self along with faith that the Holy Spirit will help one in this matter.

In an effort to define further this matter we shall look at the case of a man who experienced impulses to wrongdoing because of a lack of acceptance as a child. Gordon Larwell, a devoted and sincere Christian, went to his pastor for counsel about his strong tendency toward "ego-enhancement." He told his pastor that he had a pronounced tendency to seek preferment over others. He wished for church offices strongly and he was highly sensitive if his abilities were not recognized. He said that it seemed to him that he responded to commendation with an overly eager attitude and that he was hypersensitive to personal criticism. When criticized, even on trivial matters, he had a pronounced inclination to defend himself stoutly even in dubious situations. He often had an urge to feel depressed if people disapproved of his doings.

As Larwell discussed his situation further he pointed out some related problems. He said that he frequently sensed a temptation to conform to standards that were below his Christian ideals, particularly when he was in groups. He explained that in some situations, he was tempted to acquiesce to evil rather than to reprove it; to compromise rather than to protest. He said that he felt that his spiritual life had ambivalent urges, urges to the good and the bad.

The pastor helped this parishioner to see for the first time the meaning of some of his early childhood experiences in reference to his adult Christian life. Larwell had been brought up in a home that had deprived him of a sense of belonging and of genuine love. He thus developed early an extravagant desire to be accepted and to be loved — a heritage that God desires for every child. The acceptance by others came to be a thing he wanted and needed most. He carried this dominant want into adulthood and his religious experiences did not remove it.

The pastor pointed out that Larwell's tendencies toward self-enhancement were not necessarily rooted in sin. His strong desire for recognition, by the election to an office or otherwise, was sought so that he might assure himself that he was accepted by the group. His unfavorable response to personal criticism arose out of an unfounded fear that he was losing that which he needed most — the genuine acceptance by others. His tendencies to conform and compromise were not necessarily rooted in carnal cowardice but again were unconsciously motivated because the frustrations of early life had brought about an extravagant fear of being rejected.

It should be observed that Larwell did not commit overt sin. He did not injure others by actually seeking preferences nor did he speak bitter words to those who criticized him. His problem was inner. In times of psychic insecurity, emotions relating to inferiority feelings arose and provided impulses to "protect" himself. Christians have long called these impulses temptations.

Temptations consist, in part, of involuntary tendencies to action and of unconscious wishes. They also contain conditioned responses to situations that involve psychic danger. Moreover, Satan takes advantage of the maladjusted areas of life in temptation. He makes them a base of operations and he tempts men along the lines in which they are the weakest.

Every Christian does not have Larwell's problems because he does not have his psychic needs. However, there are

persons much like him, who, having a comprehensive understanding of themselves, open their lives to the Holy Spirit
in a great moment of faith and He resolves their difficulties
immediately.

Recognizing Spiritual Drag

Moreover, in addition to providing impulses to wrongdoing, complexes and impulses to maladjustive behavior constitute a heavy drag in Christian experience. They hinder
greatly the onward march of the Christian life. They are
psychological infirmities that hinder spiritual progress in
somewhat the same manner that bodily infirmities hinder
certain kinds of physical achievement. The anxious person,
for instance, encounters numerous frustrations because of
his unfounded and nebulous fears. He has little time or
energy to fight evil because he spends so much effort in
looking at the fearful phantoms about him and within him.
He is hindered in Christian service because of a fear of failure. He is frustrated in his life of prayer because of dis-
tracting anxieties. He is hesitant in faith, inwardly fearing
that God will not help him with his anxiety-ridden problems.
Kierkegaard pointed out in his classic work on anxiety that
dread or anxiety "is the psychological condition that pre-
cedes sin."[4]

Rationalization, as a maladjustive means of meeting problems, becomes a hindrance in the Christian life. The man
who, as a boy, developed a psychic mechanism for maintaining his self-esteem by justifying himself, no matter how great
his failures, created an impediment for the spiritual life. In
coming to adulthood, he had a well-formed pattern of looking at the contributing causes of his failure which seemed,
quite happily, to be adequate to account for his lack of success. Such a man, after conversion, finds it hard to face up
to spiritual reality. He has a well-developed habit of justifying himself instead of acknowledging his needs and failures.

[4]Soren Kierkegaard, *The Concept of Dread* (Princeton: Princeton University Press, 1944), p. 82.

He may excuse his sins as mistakes and exempt himself from the responsibility for them on the basis of human frailty. Sometimes he justifies himself on the basis of church membership instead of facing up to himself in the light of God's Word.

In like manner, the person who learns to meet problems by over-aggression encounters frustrating experiences in the Christian life. For such a man, attack seems to be the basic and, perhaps, the only solution to problems. In the Christian life, he has a tendency to attack problems in his own wisdom without seeking divine guidance. He expends human energy without seeking divine aid. He is frequently belligerent in the Christian life, demonstrating an extreme disposition to oppose all who do not agree or cooperate with him in doctrine and Christian life. Many of his attacks are ill-advised, inasmuch as they originate in a maladjustive pattern of behavior, and his zealous efforts are fruitless, or even harmful. On observing such results from his "consecrated efforts," he then suffers disillusionment and discouragement. At other times, he, like Elijah, feels alone in the Lord's battle and he becomes critical of his more deliberate brethren.

There are other forms of maladjustive behavior that constitute frustrations in the Christian life. The Christian who acquired a masochistic impulse, an unconscious wish to suffer from life's experiences, finds it difficult to accept God's forgiveness. He has an inner urge to be punished. The adult who grew up without a healthy sense of parental approval also finds it difficult to believe that God really accepts him. The overly scrupulous person, bogged down in morbid and nebulous guilt feelings, encounters a problem in maintaining a confident sense of forgiveness. He is highly sensitized to his failure in the little things of life. Moreover, he is motivated to concentrate his attention on certain minute things of the spiritual life and he thus neglects the weightier matters. The religious man who grew up with a complex of emotionally charged ideas in the area of race equality finds many of those ideas an impediment as he seeks to implement personally the New Testament teaching on brotherhood. The pampered child, early confirmed in the habit of self-reference, encounters hindering factors as he undertakes to work effectively with others.

The psychologically immature adult is not made mature suddenly in any great religious experience. He has a large assignment of make-up work to do as he seeks to take his place of responsibility in the Christian community. An increased understanding of the character and source of maladjustive behavior helps him do this. He acts constructively as he sees that maladjustments are not to be forgiven as deliberate wrongdoing, and that complexes are not cleansed as is sin. The Christian then turns to the Spirit, and perhaps to his pastor as a personal counselor, for insight into and guidance in the matter of attaining Christian maturity.

PROMOTING CHRISTIAN MATURITY

An important condition for healthful Christian growth is a genuine recognition of the fact that there is a qualitative difference between innate sin and the maladjustive impulses. The Christian who does not distinguish between these interior sources of evil faces two spiritually destructive hazards.

First, the believer may become spiritually disillusioned and give up all confidence in the phenomenon of spiritual cleansing. When he discovers that spiritual cleansing, for which he had believed, does not always remove the maladjustive impulses, as he has supposed, he may come to doubt the possibility of heart-cleansing and adjust to a life of spiritual mediocrity thinking that his spiritual condition is rooted inevitably in an unchangeable condition of human nature. Inasmuch as his inner sin and his maladjustments are confused, he neither prays for spiritual cleansing nor does he seek intelligently to resolve his maladjustments.

The other hazard is even worse. Having trusted Christ for

spiritual cleansing, the believer professes to be cleansed, but as time goes by, doubts and feelings of guilt arise. He then secretly fears that his heart has not been cleansed because of the presence of urges to wrongdoing that arise out of a dynamic core of maladjusted experiences. However, he continues to profess spiritual cleansing but it is in doubt and in insincerity. Nothing blights the spiritual life as much as an insincere profession of divine grace.[5]

Christians have a great spiritual resource for self-knowledge in the ministry of the Holy Spirit. Jesus said that He, the Holy Spirit, would guide His disciples into all truth (John 16:13). This is a continuing ministry. The Spirit leads sincere believers into truth about themselves. He personalizes truth to them. He, as the Spirit of Truth, sheds the light of His presence within their hearts, and they observe inner motives that they could have never discovered alone. Moreover, He reveals personal truth to believers in many other ways including the ministrations of the Christian church and trained therapists.

The Holy Spirit helps the Christian to identify his maladjustive impulses. This is a basic step. The identification of relevant problem areas is as important in spiritual health as it is in mental health. Little progress, for instance, can be made in the permanent recovery of mental health until one recognizes his maladjustments. Perhaps every psychiatrist has failed with some patients because they refused to look at the maladjusted areas of their lives. Likewise, the development of spiritual health depends on a clear recognition of the acquired tendencies to sub-Christian behavior.

[5]Many leaders of the deeper spiritual life recognize, quite properly, that there is a hazard in emphasizing the fact that urges to wrongdoing arise out of maladjustive experiences. They fear that such discussions as the one in this chapter immobilize people in their quest for spiritual cleansing. They are aware of the human predisposition to settle down into spiritual mediocrity, thinking of their sins as maladjustments. Perhaps the danger seems greater than it really is. The sincere of heart do not wish to rationalize their sins and the insincere cannot be coerced into holy living — not even by a rigid theology or by stringent discipline.

Every Christian should recognize the phenomenon of psychic resistance when the Holy Spirit seeks to reveal one's complexes to him. There is normally a mental set against actually accepting the fact that certain maladjustive impulses exist in him. This happens often in depth counseling. Patients often resist the recall of painful insights as the therapist tries to get them to see themselves. The same phenomenon happens in the personal ministry of the Holy Spirit. He, as the Master Counselor, helps the believer to lessen his resistance and dare to look at himself.

The importance of the Holy Spirit's assistance in getting the Christian to identify and genuinely accept his maladjustive impulses as maladjustments, and not as sin, can hardly be overemphasized. In some cases a genuine recognition of these factors opens a door that leads to Christian maturity.

The Holy Spirit, in the second place, helps the Christian to carry on remedial activities through use of spiritual resources. His leadership along this line is as varied as is His genius. We shall observe a few representative ways in which He works to bring about Christian insight and maturity.

The Holy Spirit helps the believer to acknowledge his maladjustive impulses in prayer. A healthful practice of this on occasion proves beneficial and reduces the energy of the impulses. It lessens their emotional drive. Many times this practice, through the phenomenon of answered prayer, eliminates maladjustive impulses altogether. The practice of acknowledging maladjustments in prayer can become, of course, a chronic exercise of self-pity and spiritual futility if carried on only by human initiative. The Holy Spirit saves it from that in the life of the thoughtful Christian.

The Holy Spirit also forearms the Christian for times of spiritual stress by bringing to his mind the personal realization of his maladjustive tendencies. The believer thus puts them into the equation of the situation. For example, the recognition of a personal tendency toward feelings of inferiority sometimes helps when one is tempted to be discouraged. At such times he may say, "The situation evidently is not as bad as it looks to me because I have a tendency to look at the dark side of things."

The Holy Spirit, moreover, helps Christians to grow in difficult situations. He makes the frustrating experiences of life to be constructive instead of destructive. He helps the anxiety-ridden person to grow by inspiring faith within him. He helps the one laden with morbid guilt feelings by a reaffirmation of his living relationship to Christ. He helps the Christian who tends to have a sense of futility by revealing to him the eternal significance of the Kingdom of God. The Holy Spirit helps the Christian in every difficult situation by a sense of His presence. His tutorship in the stressful situations of life brings about personal growth as it does with children who develop when they have parental guidance in situations that are difficult for them.

The Holy Spirit uses many of the constituted resources of the church in helping Christians to know themselves and to develop maturity. He makes the corporate worship services times of personal growth as He brings insights and divine grace to the worshiper. He uses the Christian fellowship groups as a resource to help individuals overcome a sense of personal isolation. He uses the service opportunities of the church as a means to achieve things for God and thus reduce the strength of the person's sense of inadequacy. He uses ministers as counselors to reveal highly relevant personal truth to individuals. He uses trained therapists to structure counseling situations so that the counselee may see himself more objectively and take constructive measures that foster maturity.

We have discussed in this chapter some of the personal values of understanding maladjustive impulses. Most of these values have related directly to the Christian's own personal growth. There is another value of high significance. An understanding of one's own maladjustments helps one to maintain confidence in his Christian brethren. The man who can look at himself without excessive rationalization and projection, is slow to think of his fellow Christians as insincere because their behavior is not perfect. A Christian, in referring to a difficult life situation that involved interpersonal tensions, said, "Had I known earlier more about the maladjustive impulses in human personality I could have worked effectively with a fellow Christian whom I came to feel was a hypocrite."

CHAPTER VI

Looking at Spiritual Frustrations

Insight into the nature of spiritual frustrations does much to assure success in the spiritual quest. A realistic attitude toward the tempting situations of life raises one's frustration tolerance, namely, the ability to accept and work through situations that threaten the spiritual life. On the other hand, a lack of insight into the spiritual hindrances leaves one unprepared to meet the obstacles. A failure to understand strategems of Satan exposes one to surprise attack, as an army that has no intelligence service.

We use the term spiritual frustration here in a twofold sense. It indicates both those factors in human personality and those situations in life that threaten the spiritual quest. In other words, we refer to basic things that thwart spiritual progress. The term "thwart" is descriptive in this connection. It suggests an obstruction that lies across the path of the one who is on the quest for spiritual reality.

In this chapter we shall observe additional inner factors along with outward situations that thwart spiritual progress. First, we shall consider the relevant physiological and constitutional factors. Second, we shall consider some of the temptations that come from the exterior environment.

The Body: Friend or Foe?

Christians from the earliest days have recognized that the human body offers impediments to spiritual progress. Thus, the spirit of man often has spoken disparagingly of the body, its earthly house. This type of talk is rather surprising in view of the fact that the spirit and body must effect a working agreement for a period of seventy years, more or less.

There have been times when the spirit of man considered the body as a friendless prison house. At other times, during the Gnostic movement for instance, man considered the body as inherently evil, as he considered all other matter. The Christian Gnostics were so completely convinced of that fact that they adjusted their theology about Christ to this one "settled" proposition. They affirmed that Jesus could not have had a real physical body while on earth because all flesh is evil. At other times in history the physiological drives, especially the sex drive, have been considered as inherently evil. Many monks, hidden away in monasteries, for example, were so opposed to the physical body with its sex urges that they became ingenious in perfecting methods of physical torment. They seemed to believe that the body was an incorrigible evildoer that deserved the most rigorous kind of abuse.

In our day we have come to think more kindly of the body, and perhaps more truly. We assert with a good deal of confidence that the body is not inherently evil, and that the physiological drives, including sex, are not bad in themselves. We believe that the physical body, rather, may be used for either good or evil. We may recruit it to support the human spirit in either evil or righteous pursuits. It will accompany the mind into evil, as a thoughtless accomplice, and indulge in experiences of sinful gratification. The hunger drive, for instance, leads sometimes to gluttony; thirst frequently leads to alcoholism; and sex sometimes becomes philandering. On the other hand, the body will stand by the aspiring mind and support it to the limit of its endurance, even offering itself in sacrifice for the convictions of the soul.

A contemporary attitude that is more favorable to the body must not obscure the fact that there are constitutional and physical factors that, while not being morally good or evil, do bring about a drag to the soul. Two classes of these will be considered here. First, there are structural factors in the human temperament that hinder spiritual progress. Second, physical and health conditions affect the spiritual life.

Temperament may be considered as an individual's constitutional tendency to react to the environment in certain ways. Some persons are more relaxed than others; some more high-strung; some more vigorous. Temperament suggests the nature of "the internal weather" that characterizes an individual. There are people who are normally placid while others are turbulent.

Temperament appears to be an inborn tendency which is the result of the chemical and metabolic processes in the body. These processes do much to determine one's change of mood. They are significant in conditioning his outlook on life. They affect strongly his emotional responses. They help pattern the kind of responses that he will make to the demands of life. Temperament does much to determine the individual differences in people. "It is unlikely that a constitutionally phlegmatic individual would develop an anxious, rigid, and compulsive character structure."[1] Likewise, it is not highly probable that the child with a choleric temperament will develop into a passive and easygoing person. Most parents, having been nonplussed by the different reactions of their children to similar situations, agree with the scientists who deal with this matter that inherited temperamental factors are pretty important in life.

Some of the temperamental traits greatly help in the spiritual life, while others hinder. Our primary interest here is in the latter.

The person with the *phlegmatic* temperament, to use the old Greek category of temperaments, encounters a problem in the area of Christian activity and service. He has a disposition to be passive in the Christian life; to become a little

[1]Leland E. Henzie and Robert J. Campbell, *Psychiatric Dictionary* (New York: Oxford University Press, 1953), p. 726.

nonfunctioning "saint" who wishes to enjoy the comforts and securities of the Christian life, but who is not disposed to contribute vigorously to its ongoing. He has a disposition to be more interested in Sunday school picnics than in holy crusades.

The person with a *melancholic* temperament encounters a problem in the area of spiritual discouragement. With an inborn tendency for depression, he may lose his enthusiasm for Christ when the going is hard. He is tempted strongly to give up the spiritual quest in such an hour.

The Christian with the *choleric* temperament meets a problem in the matter of patience. Living an inwardly intense life, he is predisposed to be impatient and angry with those who do not agree or cooperate with him. He also has a tendency to surrender his faith when he must wait long for the development of spiritual plans or the appearance of anticipated values.

Many Christians with *sanguine* temperaments, in spite of all their delightful cheerfulness, tend to lack inner stability. Sometimes they seem to live on the surface of life with enthusiasms that are short-lived. Jesus spoke of this class of people in the Parable of the Soils, when He referred to those who received the word with great joy but, "lacking root within themselves," soon forsook the truth they had so happily embraced.

Second, in addition to temperament, physical and health conditions often constitute situations that become spiritually frustrating. A person with a pronounced physical handicap, the loss of one leg for instance, may stumble over the question of "how a good God could let a thing like this happen to me." The difficult situation may become a stumbling block instead of a steppingstone to new victory — a cause of defeat instead of a challenge to richer spiritual life.

Moreover, the doctors inform us that many illnesses have factors that become religiously frustrating. Some illnesses cause marked depressions, others bring about inner tensions and stresses, and still others lower physical vigor so greatly that one feels incapacitated to encounter life's problems. Likewise, some of the rather constant physical conditions may have considerable spiritual relevance. Sometimes low blood pressure contributes to depression, and high blood pressure to an inner intensity, both of which have spiritual relevance.

Spiritual health is also affected through the improper day to day care of the body. Both body and soul become sluggish through a lack of physical exercise. On the other hand, overwork makes a dull spirit, if we are to believe the lines about Jack who had "all work and no play." The lack of sleep through the keeping of irregular hours reduces physical, mental, and spiritual effectiveness. Overeating can likewise affect one's spiritual perspective, changing it from hope to a sense of defeat.

The account is given of a frontier circuit preacher, hungry and tired, who went to a home of Christian people to stay all night. Before he went to bed he entered an optimistic note in his diary.

> Arrived at the home of Brother Brown late this evening, hungry and tired after a long day in the saddle. Had a bountiful supper of cold pork and beans, warm bread, bacon and eggs, coffee and rich pastry. I go to rest feeling that my witness is clear; the future is bright; I feel called to a great and glorious work in this place. Brother Brown's family are godly people.

On the basis of his entry the next morning before he left his room, it appears that his "bountiful supper" had changed his spiritual outlook.

> Awakened late this morning after a troubled night. I am very much depressed in soul; the way looks dark; far from being called to work among this people, I am beginning to doubt the safety of my soul. I am afraid that the desires of Brother Brown and his family are set too much on carnal things.[2]

2Leslie R. Marston, *From Chaos to Character* (Winona Lake, Ind.: Light and Life Press, 1937), pp. 76-77.

TEMPTATION: VICTORY OR DEFEAT

Deterministic theories about human nature have disarmed modern man against temptation, robbing him of his sense of moral strength. Man has resigned the captaincy of his soul in believing these theories. These erroneous theories have weakened him by giving him a rationalization for his moral failures. In accepting a deterministic hypothesis, man believes that he is overcome by the irresistible forces of human impulse. Modern man often surrenders to his id, to those inner instinctual drives that motivate toward pleasure.

Deterministic theories about the effect of environment on human behavior have also robbed man at times of the real captaincy of his soul. Men have capitulated easily to social forces because they had become supine in believing that they could not withstand them.

Temptation is usually composed of both inner dispositions to do wrong and outer circumstances that invite evil-doing. The interior evil dispositions ally themselves with the exterior sensuous environment in an effort to defeat the high aspirations of the soul. Every person on the spiritual quest needs to recognize this confederacy that is bent on leading him into sin.

Temptation is a time of crisis to every man. From the temptation he will emerge a victor or a victim. The temptation will prove to be the occasion of personal triumph or of spiritual tragedy. Our interest here is primarily how one may make temptations a time of personal growth.

Temptation under the superintendence of God becomes a means of spiritual grace and power. Victory in temptation brought the ministry of angels to Jesus (Matthew 4:11). He returned from His temptation in the wilderness "in the power of the Spirit into Galilee, and a report concerning Him went out through all the surrounding country" (Luke 4:14, R.S.V.). Paul said that he was made strong through the tempting things of life — "weaknesses, insults, hardships, persecutions, and calamities" (II Corinthians 12:10, r.s.v.). James told his readers to "Count it all joy, . . . when you meet various trials, (often a temptation) for you know that the testing of your faith produces steadfastness" (James 1:2, 3, r.s.v.).

Much spiritual growth comes in the crises of life, both small and great. Spiritual growth tends to be by leaps, as does mental growth. In temptation, we gain insights that lift us to new levels of life. In temptation, we draw upon resources of divine power that we did not know existed. In temptation, we make commitments to God that strengthen life. We learn watchfulness in temptation. We learn that temptation helps deliver us from human pride and arrogant self-dependence. Paul said that his thorn in the flesh helped save him from pride. George Eliot said that "No one is well matriculated to the art of life till he has been well-tempted." Lowell stated that one "learns more metaphysics from a single temptation than from all the philosophies."

The Bible, in contrast to much contemporary literature, strengthens men to encounter temptation through its realistic treatment of the human situation. It represents a legacy of spiritual energy rather than one of moral languor and lassitude. It views the evil environment, the world, fearlessly, but it assures man of victory. It believes that man, by the grace of God, can go in the right direction even in evil days.

The Bible leaves no room for the conscious mind to surrender to the unconscious forces of life. It is realistic about the power of human drives, but it confidently offers a solution.

The Bible strengthens men in that it helps them recognize that temptation is the lot of all people. Even Jesus "was led up of the spirit into the wilderness to be tempted of the devil" (Matthew 4:1). Nowhere does the Bible suggest that God will exempt His children from temptation. Peter exhorted his readers not to be "surprised at the fiery ordeal which comes upon you to prove you, as though something strange were happening to you" (I Peter 4:12, R.S.V.).

The Bible strengthens men by warning them that Satan is a strategist in tempting men. "Put on the whole armor of God, that you may be able to stand against the wiles of the devil" (Ephesians 6:11, R.S.V.). Like a master tactician, Satan attacks humankind at its weakest point. The Bible, as the instructions of a great army general, suggests that one should never underestimate the strategy of the enemy.

The Satanic strategy often has a long perspective. Satan has learned in his long experience of tempting men that it often pays to work slowly and subtly. He thus undertakes to undermine the strongholds of character through compromises in the thought life. He seeks to stimulate a sinful imagination in areas of sex, avarice, and resentment, knowing that inner thoughts become overt acts. One of the central teachings of Jesus was that inner thought life must be kept pure.

The Bible strengthens men by making it clear that God has not capitulated to the forces of evil as have, it seems, some contemporary psychologists. He defines the limits to which Satan can go in the human situation of temptation. "No temptation has overtaken you that is not common to man. God is faithful, and he will not let you be tempted beyond your strength, but with the temptation will also provide the way of escape, that you may be able to endure it" (I Corinthians 10:13, R.S.V). God's concern for His tempted children is in the Incarnation. Christ pioneered the way to perfect obedience through suffering and temptation. "For because he himself (Christ) has suffered and been tempted, he is able to help those who are tempted" (Hebrews 2:18, R.S.V.).

God does something better than provide exemption from temptation. He promises divine strength for personal victory over it. Paul prayed earnestly for the removal of the thorn in his flesh. God did not remove the thorn but He said, "My grace is sufficient for you, for my power is made perfect in weakness" (II Corinthians 12:9, R.S.V.).

Two principles are basic to the matter of meeting spiritual frustrations. First, man must maintain a sense of personal responsibility. He must not surrender his soul to his drives. Neither can he be saved by sitting on the sidelines of life expecting a kindly Providence to defend him from all evil. The spiritual life demands that one maintain the captaincy of his soul under God. The man has capitulated spiritually who says, "It's not my fault. How can I be held responsible for all of my acts if God made me this way and put me in this kind of a world?" The second principle is a confident trust in God for help. This means that there must be a wholesome synthesis of reliance on self and dependence upon God. Success does not come to the jaunty fellow who feels that he has all of the answers and that he is able to handle the situation himself. Without divine wisdom and help he falls into one temptation after another.

CHAPTER VII

Cultivating the Christian Life

The Christian, as the athlete, must carry on faithfully those arts and practices that make him strong and efficient. In line with this emphasis, the Revised Standard Version translates I Timothy 4:7b, "Train yourself in godliness." The word "train" in the Greek text is an athletic term that means "to exercise vigorously." It may be used to suggest spiritual, physical, or mental exercise. Phillips, in his interpretative translation of this verse, says, "Take the time and trouble to keep yourself spiritually fit."

A famous football coach, "Hurry-up" Yost, formerly of the University of Michigan, once rebuked a confident player who said that their team would win because it had "the will to win."

"Don't fool yourself," said Yost. "The will to win isn't worth a nickel unless you have the will to prepare."[1]

Success in the Christian life depends heavily upon the willingness to cultivate it. There are numerous exercises in it that are helpful. We shall note three of these in this chapter.

KNOWING THE TEXTBOOK

The Bible is the textbook on the science and art of living. It sets forth the basic principles of effective living as surely as a textbook in geometry sets forth basic principles of

[1]Halford Luccock, in *The Christian Herald*, January, 1959, p. 42.

mathematics. Paul is explicit in stating this to be the purpose of the Bible. "All Scripture is given by inspiration of God, and is profitable for doctrine, for reproof, for correction, for instruction in righteousness: That the man of God may be perfect, throughly furnished unto all good works" (II Timothy 3:16, 17).

The Bible is a book about life, drawing large portions of its materials from actual life experiences. Its characters were not make-believe personages or fictitious men and women stepping out upon an imaginary stage in an effort to dramatize life. They were actual men and women who encountered the rugged facts of life. They were not starry-eyed idealists speaking out of a poverty of experience in an attempt to give guidance to nonplussed mortals. Rather, they were real persons, hard pressed at times, who met the same kind of frustrations and problems that confront men today.

The Bible, moreover, is more than a record of man's moral experiments. It is a book of human experience under divine evaluation and criticism. It contains the record of God's judgment on both the bad and the good. It portrays, on the one hand, the failure of evil conduct. King Saul shouts across the centuries with tragic eloquence that divine rejection finally follows disobedience of God (I Samuel 28:15). David tells all men convincingly that adultery brings self-disillusionment and a loss of divine favor (Psalm 51:1-17). Peter says that bitter tears follow betrayal of Christ. On the other hand, the Bible portrays the success of righteous conduct. The record of a tempted Joseph in Potiphar's house, proclaims eloquently that God honors loyalty to conviction, even in a strange city. David and Jonathan declare that God approves men who regard friendship of greater worth than selfish ambitions. Ruth counsels all women that God esteems loyalty in love. In these instances, and in many others, the Bible reports the experiments that demonstrated the validity of righteous living as surely as Euclid demonstrated the truth of certain geometric hypotheses. It shows the error of wrong life-hypotheses by writing out the equation in terms of human failure.

The Bible, as a record of human experience under divine judgment, is the basis for a personal evaluation of life. To change the figure, its vivid materials reflect, like a mirror, the moral image of the man who looks into it with spiritual honesty. Sometimes one is surprised at the personal moral image which he sees when he looks into the Scriptures. One is often like Lincoln who first looked into a mirror when he was a lad. Upon seeing his reflection, he exclaimed, "Is that *me?*"

Self-evaluation in the light of God's standard, is essential if there is to be spiritual progress. The ability to see one's self is necessary for religious achievement as well as for every other endeavor. Failure in self-evaluation spells futility in our efforts. The public press has recently reported that Helen Traubel, one-time singing instructor to a well-known young woman, stated that her student "failed because she had no gift of self-criticism."

Three basic attitudes toward the Bible are essential if it is to provide us with an effective means of self-evaluation.

First, we must read the Bible with confidence, believing that it is the Word of God. The Bible becomes an inspired Book to the man who believes it is inspired of God. Thus, believing that it is God's wisdom about human existence, he is willing to risk his life on its precepts. He believes that it is authoritative, even when contradicted by certain theories in contemporary psychology, many of which will soon pass away as the grass and stubble.

The Bible becomes a relevantly inspired book to the man who believes that human nature does not change through the centuries, and that human problems remain basically the same. It becomes a timely book to the man who believes that a sinful world presents the same basic problem to men in every age. This problem, seen from the days of Eden, is the temptation to turn from eternal values to transient satisfactions, satisfactions rooted in sensate wishes and in human pride. The Bible becomes more relevant for life than the latest book in psychology to the man who believes that it contains divine wisdom about human nature and experience. The Scriptures are a basis for self-evaluation when a man believes that they "evoke the dimensions of the total self: emotion and thought, joy and sorrow, loneliness and comradeship, fear and deliverance, pugnacity and tenderness, the hunger for beauty and truth."[2]

Second, we must read the Bible with an objectivity about self. There is no place for "proof texting" rationalizations for one's failure when one reads the Scriptures. Impulses to justify one's self through rationalization should be recognized and renounced when one reads God's Word. This calls for a high degree of spiritual sincerity which expresses itself in a moral courage to look at one's spiritual disfigurements and blemishes. It represents a realistic attitude toward self like the one that was expressed by Cromwell, who had a large wart on his face, when he said to his portrait artist, "Paint me just as I am, wart and all."

Third, we must read the Bible with a practical attitude, with a spirit of personal quest for light on living. We need to say, "Light, more light," as we read. The Greek philosopher, Diogenes, with his lantern in hand should symbolize our search for truth. We need the patient spirit of the philosopher searching for the meaning of things, and the critical spirit of the scientist as he carries on his research.

We must relate the truth of the Scriptures to our lives if we are to make Bible study practical. "Let us read the Bible thinking constantly of our daily lives and let us live our lives thinking constantly of the Bible."[3]

The study of the Scriptures is of crucial importance in

[2]Ernest L. Talbert, in "Foreword," Abraham Cronbach's *The Realities of Religion* (New York: Bookman Associates, 1957), p. vii.

[3]A statement that Emil Brunner made in conversation with Paul Tournier, in Paul Tournier's, *A Doctor's Casebook in the Light of the Bible* (London: S. C. M. Press, 1954), p. 18.

the Christian life. Much sin is the result of personal ignorance concerning God's revealed will. Peter speaks of a self-chosen and personally approved ignorance that results from the neglect of the Word of God (II Peter 3:5). Such ignorance, usually consisting of an incoherent smattering of religious truth, represents a nonchalance about God's standard of righteousness. It is the living incarnation of the words of the wicked. "Therefore they say unto God, Depart from us; for we desire not the knowledge of thy ways" (Job 21:14). Self-chosen ignorance is a cause of sin. Hosea says in plaintive tones, "My people are destroyed for lack of knowledge: because thou hast rejected knowledge, I will also reject thee, . . . seeing thou hast forgotten the law of thy God, I will also forget thy children" (Hosea 4:6). Jeremiah contrasts confused man, in a state of willful ignorance, to God's creatures that obey the laws of nature.

> Even the stork in the heavens knows her times:
> and the turtledove, swallow, and crane
> keep the time of their coming;
> but my people know not
> the ordinance of the Lord.
>   (Jeremiah 8:7, R.S.V.)

Jesus recognized ignorance as the cause of wrongdoing. "Ye do err, not knowing the scriptures, nor the power of God" (Matthew 22:29).

PERSONALIZING CORPORATE WORSHIP

Genuine worship is a highly personal matter whether it takes place in a congregation or alone. It is, in its truest sense, the individual's thoughtful response to God in a super-sensory form of divine-human communication. In this meeting between God and man, God comes to our aid with all the grace we need and we, in turn, reach toward Him with thankful, committed, and receptive attitudes. This divine-human meeting may take place anywhere. It may be in a great cathedral thronged with people, in a small group gathered in a country church, in a family circle as it turns to worship, or when one is alone. The divine-human meeting is unseen by others, even by those who may be at one's side.

It is axiomatic, of course, that one may participate in exercises of worship without making worship personal. A printed page instead of a devoted heart may be the motivation of hallowed words that are spoken as the current of the worship service bears one along. One may say prayers without praying. In doing this, one becomes an impersonal actor in a religious drama that has little meaning to him.

The man on the spiritual quest personalizes his worship in the congregation. He recognizes, in the first place, that nothing will be done automatically for him merely because the minister speaks sacred words and performs religious acts. He recognizes that spiritual health insurance cannot be purchased by putting money in the offering plate as can life insurance be bought at the air terminal by putting quarters in a machine. Moreover, he guards against the routinization of the service knowing that words become threadbare through usage and that living truths become entombed in familiar phrases.

The questing spirit guards against the spiritual hazards of corporate worship. With an open mind and a seeking heart man prepares the way for a divine-human encounter. He makes the words of the liturgy his own; he responds with an inward "amen" to the petitions; he relates the truth of the sermon to his own life.

The man with a questing attitude for spiritual reality is aware of the phenomenon of religious ambivalence. He knows that one may feel kindly toward God, especially in the presence of sacred things, and at the same time love the ways of the world. He knows that one may both love and hate his evil ways. The sincere worshiper thus avoids superficial repentance when he senses the rise of religious aspiration in the worship service.

The man who personalizes worship does not substitute symbols for reality nor liturgy for religious vitality. He is not highly suggestible concerning himself when the minister, with a kindly overgeneralization, refers to the congregation as "persons who are devoted to Christ." He knows that every man must stand on his own feet before God. Naturally he wishes to be a Christian but he does not permit wishful thinking to obscure his vision of personal spiritual needs.

Hunger for God helps a man avoid the peril of rationalization. The man who wants spiritual reality does not try to justify himself with dubious evidence. Neither does he engage in compensations, trying to exchange some good thing for God's favor. The service closes for such a man with a new sense of strength because he has been more than a member of an audience, more than a passive listener; he has been a participant with God in a living situation. The hour of worship is for him a time of mental alertness and spiritual alacrity as he considers the eternal things. It is his best hour of the week.

There are those in our day who are overly dependent upon the Sunday morning worship service for their spiritual health. They make this the primary, if not the sole, religious exercise of their lives. Dependence upon a worship service is insufficient, as valuable as it is. To do so is like a sick man trying to regain health by listening once a week to a lecture on medicine. He must come to know that his case demands personal and continued attention. Then under a doctor's guidance he can devote personal care to his health problem.

The questing spirit often has led Christians to seek out small groups of like-minded persons for an informal type of worship that gave large place to personal expression. For instance, the early Christians, drawn together as by a spiritual magnet, gathered in the homes of fellow believers to sing hymns, offer prayers, exchange Christian experiences, and break bread in commemoration of Christ's death. The

Moravians gathered in small groups to search the Scriptures, pray, and testify of God's goodness. The Methodists originated the class meetings, limited to twelve persons in Wesley's day. In these meetings, they told frankly of their spiritual experiences, praising God for victories and speaking specifically of their frustrations.

The value of small groups of informal worshipers throughout Christian history is immeasurable. After years of perspective on the class meetings, Wesley said that it could "scarcely be conceived what advantages had been reaped" from them.[4]

The significance of small-group worship is seen more clearly today than ever before. A number of contemporary disciplines have confirmed the values of it. Psychiatry and clinical psychology use small groups in group therapy to assist persons to gain insight into themselves and their problems. Social psychology authenticates small-group worship by its emphasis on the values of social interaction in small groups. Educational theory, in its emphasis on group dynamics, attests small-group worship by demonstrating that insights and incentives come when persons are together in a mutual and meaningful situation.

The contempory church offers numerous opportunities for spiritual nurture in small groups. There are groups for prayer and for Bible study. There are youth groups and adult Christian interest groups. All of these offer opportunities for personal expression and insight.

Moreover, the questing spirit leads many earnest seekers for spiritual reality to a vital form of family worship. Such a practice is rooted in the command of God to Israel: "and you shall teach them (the divine commandments) diligently to your children, and shall talk of them when you sit in your house, and when you walk by the way, and when

[4]John Wesley, *Letters,* Standard Edition, John Telford, editor (London: Epworth Press, 1931), Vol. II, p. 297.

you lie down, and when you rise" (Deuteronomy 6:7 r.s.v.). God ordained that the commandments, and worship more largely, should be an integral and not a peripheral part of life. He wished worship rooted in the common daily practices of life. Israel responded to this command of God better than have most of the Christians, and the continuity of the Hebrew race and religion, as a rare phenomenon of history under the most difficult circumstances, is a strong commendation of the divine wisdom in ordaining family religion.

Family worship is a form of group worship *par excellence.* It has a built-in personal factor based in the concern and love the members of the family have for each other. It is practical because it leads to the solution of practical life problems. It is relevant inasmuch as it relates, most naturally, to all of the affairs of daily life. It is timely in that it tends to make all of life sacred in days when the secular spirit threatens all values.

MAKING PRIVATE PRAYER CREATIVE

Prayer, like every other gift of God, may be used either creatively or destructively. It may become a means of spiritual growth or a means to stunt spiritual development. It may help lift life to new spiritual heights or help keep it on flatlands. Prayer is constructive if it becomes a means of meeting life creatively; it is destructive if it is used as an attempted means of escaping life. It is helpful if it represents commitment to God-appointed experiences; it is harmful if it is an urgent plea for an exemption from those experiences.

Creative prayer is characterized by a twofold achievement. First, it enriches the life of the one who prays. It inspires insights, purifies sentiments, creates new ideals, breaks the power of frustrating habits, changes purposes, and strengthens generally the life of the believer. Second, it brings about spiritual results in the environment. Answers to creative prayer are objective in that God's power is expressed in other persons who change their intents and purposes because of the working of the Holy Spirit. There are, as with every spiritual achievement, basic conditions for this type of praying.

First, a healthy balance of praise and petition is essential to creative prayer. Praise is the best auxiliary of petitions. Paul told the Philippians to mingle praise and petition when they prayed. "With thanksgiving let your request be made known to God" (Philippians 4:6). The element of thanksgiving has always been prominent in the prayers of the saints. Praise is still a good criterion of spiritual mindedness and prayer effectiveness.

Praise is essential in prayer because God's blessings put the recipient under bond. If man does not recognize God's gifts with thankfulness, he disqualifies himself, both psychologically and spiritually, to receive other gifts. The ungrateful man prays timidly, and perhaps apologetically, knowing that he is selfish in seeking divine favors and he recognizes that he has not paid his bond of gratitude. He is like a man with an overdue and unpaid loan at the bank. Such a man returns timidly, if at all, to that bank in search of additional funds.

Praise provides perspective in prayer. It delivers one from a debilitating sense of human inadequacy as one recognizes the divine-human partnership in which he is engaged. The perplexing trivialities of life appear small as one views them against the background of God as the Giver of every good gift. This perspective helps deliver one from a problem-consciousness to a power-consciousness. Praise is the best form of positive thinking.

Praise inspires faith for the petitions that one makes in prayer. "He who most bears in mind what has been done for him by God will be most emboldened to ask for great gifts from above." Praise inspires faith because it is an anti-dote to depression and anxiety. It furthermore dispels Satanic doubts. Satan has never liked praise meetings, individual or corporate. He does not like to hear God magnified.

The writer of the book of II Chronicles gives a superbly fine account of how God helps those who turn to Him in praise. "And when they (Jehoshaphat and the people of Judah) began to sing and to praise, the Lord set ambush-ments against the men of Ammon, Moab, and Mount Seir (Judah's enemies), which were come against Judah, and they were smitten" (II Chronicles 20:22).

Praise brings an exhilaration of life which releases con-structive energies. It delivers one from a sense of futility — the seedbed of lassitude and inactivity. It enlists spiritual and mental energies through the recall of past victories. It delivers from egocentricity and the sense of defeat that comes from a feeling of working alone. Praise is, like prayer itself, one of the great constructive energies of life.

Second, a personal sense of mutuality with God is essen-tial to creative prayer. Here mutuality suggests that one has a body of common interests with God; that he has adopted divine objectives; and that there are reciprocal activities between his Maker and himself. A sense of mutuality is the basis for spiritual fellowship. It makes prayer "conversation with God," as Clement of Alexandria said.

Prayer, without an identity of interests with God, is a type of spiritual exploitation. It represents an attempt to wrest things from the Almighty by "the magic of prayer" without offering ourselves in return. It is an effort to enrich self at God's expense. Being alienated from God, one prays in an endeavor to obtain divine blessings and use them for self.

Rufus Jones says that one of the primary dangers of prayer is the utilitarian spirit. This is especially true in sensate days such as our own. The world and the church are filled with people who pray "give-me" prayers. This is one reason for the extensive spiritual dearth that exists today. One strikes at the very heart of spiritual religion when one tries to make prayer a short cut by which he can aggrandize himself.

Third, an attitude of personal sacrifice is another essential of creative prayer. God united sacrifice and prayer in the Old Testament plan of worship and He has never separated them. The Hebrew people in the old dispensation presented offerings when they worshiped God in the temple. It cost them something to pray — a burnt offering, a sin offering, or an offering of another kind.

Let no man put sacrifice and prayer asunder. The two are joined in the Christian faith as surely as in Judaism. "I appeal to you therefore, brethren, by the mercies of God, to present your bodies as a living sacrifice, holy and acceptable to God, which is your spiritual worship" (Romans 12:1, R.S.V.). Paul infers that the Christian religion demands a more excellent sacrifice than do other religions. One must give himself, instead of things, if his worship is to be spiritual.

We may say in a dangerous partial truth that our words are "sacrifices of praise" to God. They are such if indeed they come from sacrificial attitudes. If they do not, they are cheap and spurious substitutes, totally unacceptable to God. Words can be the cheapest of all commodities in the world. One can buy fifty thousand of them at a newsstand for ten cents. Words of worship that lack a spirit of personal sacrifice and commitment to God are cheaper than that.

The emphasis that personal sacrifice and prayer must go together is a hard truth for a generation of go-getters trained in attitudes of acquisition. We seek to apply the profit motive in our dealing with God. Our practice of "giving" is often motivated by a desire of "getting." The word sacrifice seems archaic to us; it seems stored away in the archives of our lives.

Fourth, a confidence that God is an all-powerful Father is an essential of creative prayer. The one who prays effectively believes two things about God. First, he believes that He desires to give good things to His children. This is simply believing in the Fatherhood of God. Second, he believes that God is able to provide the things He wishes to give to those who ask Him. This refers to a confidence in God's power. These two elements of faith unite divine benevolence and power; a fatherly concern with divine capacity; and attitudes of love with ability. Prayer is a crippled thing if confidence is weak in either its sense of divine fatherhood or power.

Jesus gave the greatest attention to emphasizing that God was a loving Heavenly Father to every individual. The clarity of His teaching on this truth was something new on the earth. Men in earlier times viewed God as a Father of nations, but most rarely as a Father of the individual person. Jesus set forth God as Father of the individual person in unforgettable words. He said that God was concerned personally for even the birds of the air, noting the fall of the least of them. "Are ye not much better than they?" (Matthew 6:26b). He said further that our heavenly Father far exceeded our concept of earthly fathers. "If ye then being evil, know how to give good gifts to your children, how much more shall your Father which is in heaven give good things to them that ask him" (Matthew 7:11).

The Lord's Prayer emphasizes the necessity of viewing God as an all-powerful Father. It starts with the salutation, "Our Father." It ends with an ascription of His power, "For thine is the kingdom, and the power, and the glory." All of the petitions are between the salutation that denotes fatherly benevolence and the ascription that affirms the ability to provide.

The effective Christian life is always the result of divine-human cooperation. Man must train himself in Christian living; God must supplement the human training with His own working. Paul sets forth this principle in a classic statement: "Work out your own salvation with fear and trembling. For it is God which worketh in you both to will and to do of his good pleasure" (Philippians 2:12b, 13). This twofold action is as necessary for the Christian as it is for the gardener. The gardener tills the soil but it is God who gives the harvest.

CHAPTER VIII

Maintaining Healthful Attitudes

Spiritual attitudes represent the posture of the soul. They are the mental dispositions that determine the character and quality of conduct. They are the states of readiness to act positively or negatively toward persons, things and ideas. Attitudes are the real springs of action. Healthy spiritual attitudes go far in assuring success in the spiritual quest.

KEEPING AN ATTITUDE OF PERSONAL RESPONSIBILITY

Contemporary man has been reluctant to maintain an attitude of personal responsibility for his soul. As with Adam, the human race has had an enduring tendency to put the blame for wrongdoing on someone else. "The woman whom thou gavest to be with me, she gave me of the tree, and I did eat" (Genesis 3:12b). In his sense of moral responsibility, modern man is something like the schoolboy who took a poor report card home to his disapproving parents. In an ingenious attempt at self-defense, he explained, "Someone goofed; I'm not properly motivated."

The problem of motivation is, indeed, basic to the matter of personal responsibility. Many in our generation have followed seriously the behavioristic suggestion that man is of necessity a responding mechanism to the stimuli that play upon him. Large numbers have ascribed all personal qualities to heredity and environment. In accepting the behavioristic formula, $H \times E = P$, i.e., heredity times environment equals personality, these people have taken an exemption from personal accountability. They recognize that they have no responsibility for their heredity and they believe that they have little for their environment.

There are those in our generation who have surrendered their sense of personal responsibility because of their conditioned reflexes. Environment, they say, has conditioned their reflexes to make the kind of responses that they make. They thus live by their reflexes and not by reflection; by conditioning and not by choice.

Depth psychology, in addition to Behaviorism, has diminished man's sense of personal responsibility. Psychoanalysis suggests that the innate and instinctual urges — the wicked id — are so strong that man cannot hope to resist or control them. It has seemed to many that the drives within man will inevitably defeat him spiritually. These viewpoints have caused man to excuse and to pamper himself. He has surrendered easily before the threatening power of his impulses. He has given up to his complexes without a stiff moral battle. He has stood disarmed before his maladjustments rather than face up to them in the strength of inner resolution and insight. Kinsey-like, he has excused moral failures on the basis of his sex drive, forgetting that God provides resources for the control of all the impulses.

There are others who have sought an escape from a sense of moral responsibility by overemphasizing some of the other suggestions of depth psychology. They have considered themselves to be the victims of their repressions. Others have slackened their pace toward a sense of responsible selfhood because of unfavorable childhood experiences. They have remained in a state of adult immaturity because they had a mother who pampered them, or a father who dominated them, or a friend who betrayed them. There are those who overemphasize the importance of childhood traumatic experiences. They look to the destructive power of these rather than to the constructive power of insight.

Certain sociological theories have also reduced man's sense of responsibility. The urban sociologist has sometimes said, at least by inference, that a dilapidated area of a city will necessarily dilapidate a man's spirit. Rural sociologists have seemed to suggest that poor and eroding soil will necessarily erode a man's soul. Many sociological theories suggest that a man is not really responsible for the set of his soul, that unfavorable social influences and pressures are responsible. Man is moulded necessarily by his contacts. Thus, man has, in many instances, capitulated to his environment instead of reconstructing it. He has sometimes turned his soul's welfare over to his environment in a sense of personal lassitude.

Moreover, certain theological theories have immobilized man in a responsible quest for spiritual health and vigor. Some theologies have had a casual attitude toward sin. They have considered it a type of innate weakness, an inevitable part of the human situation about which man could do little or nothing. This has caused man to consider his sins as unavoidable maladjustments which God understands and accepts.

The man who has a nonchalant attitude toward his sins is immobilized in his efforts to gain spiritual health. He is like the fellow who had a chronic headache for many years. He took the headache for granted, accepting it as a part of his condition. He recognized that the distress was annoying and debilitating, but he didn't see his doctor because he had little faith in his ability to help him and, after all, he assumed that he would not die because of his aching head. He deprived himself of the possibility of robust health because he took no personal initiative for a cure.

CONSERVING ENERGY THROUGH SINCERITY

Sincerity is moral honesty; insincerity is a calculated deceit. Sincerity represents a disposition to demonstrate truth; insincerity represents a decision to live a lie and to parade falsehood. Sincerity undertakes to perform what one professes, but its counterpart is professing more than one performs. The sincere man accepts himself as he is, but the hypocrite creates a phantom self with which he wishes to meet the public. Hypocrisy is the rejection of real life and the choice of an actor's part in a drama that has upon it the marks of the spurious.

1. *Sincerity is essential to spiritual health because it establishes a basis for spiritual fellowship.* Fellowship with other Christians is an important condition for the spiritual life. Isolated saints are a rare species and, if found, they are usually dwarfed.

Honesty is an indispensable prerequisite for every group. It is necessary for fellowship. Insincerity destroys the basis for fellowship more effectively than many other sins. The gospels suggest that Jesus ate more frequently with the publicans and sinners than with the pretending Pharisees.

Insincerity destroys fellowship because the insincere man insults the intelligence of others by assuming that he is deceiving them. Forgetting that interpersonal communication is more than verbal, the hypocrite unknowingly reveals himself while continuing to act like he had deceived his friends. Fellowship cannot thrive in such a situation. None of us likes to be considered as slow-witted or as deficient concerning others.

Without Christian fellowship, the insincere man undertakes to go it alone. He is cut off from divine guidance and strength because of his hypocrisies. He deprives himself of human counsel, ever fearing to receive it lest his pretenses be discovered. He denies himself spiritual comradeship because he is going in the wrong direction. He seeks and receives little friendly assistance because of his proud heart.

2. *Sincerity fosters spiritual growth because it opens the whole heart to truth.* Truth is the life-giving substance of the Christian personality. Like a hospitable host, sincerity welcomes new truth and makes it feel at home. Likewise, it

treats the old truths so kindly that they remain in the life and operate with maximum efficiency.

Insincerity, on the other hand, is inhospitable to new truth. It fears self-discovery. It shuts off parts of the personality, like locked rooms in a house, and it carefully guards them. It turns away the Spirit of Truth Himself, the Holy Spirit, as a poor but arrogant man turns from his home a benefactor who seeks to bring food to his hungry family.

Sincerity is essential for the very existence of truth in the life. The mind loses its power to discriminate between truth and error as it juggles right and wrong. It no longer seeks truth. If it asks questions it is not in a search for truth but it is seeking an opportunity to refute it (John 9:27-28). "When the soul does not live in its own truth, the vision of God's truth also becomes clouded, for spiritual disease involves our whole thinking, our feeling and willing and even what our senses perceive."[1] Sincerity leads to a heightened sensitivity to truth while pretense dulls the spiritual senses. Sincerity has no "pride system" to maintain and no narcissistic love of self. Sincerity is able to accept itself, knowing that there are vast areas of life needing improvement.

3. *Sincerity fosters spiritual growth because all of the energy is directed toward its development.* The whole personality cooperates in this endeavor. No parts of the personality need spend time in guarding secretly locked doors. Or, to change the figure, time and energy are not spent in futile parading.

Anne Morrow Lindbergh speaks of the tiring effect of pretense:

> I find that I am shedding hypocrisy in human relationships. What a rest that will be! The most exhausting thing in life, I have discovered, is being insincere. That is why so much social life is exhausting; one is wearing a mask. I have shed my mask.[2]

[1]Josef Goldbrunner, *Holiness Is Wholeness* (New York: Pantheon, 1955), p. 32.

[2]Anne Morrow Lindbergh, *Gift from the Sea* (New York: Pantheon Books, Inc., 1955), p. 32.

T. S. Eliot expresses graphically the futility of expending energy in insincere thought.

> In the small circle of pain within the skull
> You shall tramp and tread one endless round
> Of thought, to justify your action to yourselves,
> Weaving a fiction which unravels as you weave,
> Pacing forever the hell of make-believe
> Which never is belief. . . .[3]

The hypocrite resists all efforts for his deliverance. He is well-barricaded in his citadel of deception which he built at great personal cost. J. R. Seeley calls insincerity "the one incurable vice." Even the Almighty is pictured as giving up the effort to save men who "changed the truth of God into a lie" (Romans 1:25a). When men surrender the love of truth, God sends them "an inward working of delusion." J. B. Mozley underscores the difficulty of seeing the insincere converted.

> The victim of passion then may be converted, the gay, the thoughtless, or the ambitious . . . they may be converted, any one of these—but who is to convert the hypocrite? He does not know he is a hypocrite. . . The greater hypocrite he is, the more sincere he must think himself.[4]

ADVANCING THROUGH ASPIRATION

Aspiration is a part of the driving force back of the attitude to seek spiritual reality. The Christian disposition to seek religious values is motivated by an aspiring attitude that moves one toward luminous goals. Aspiration is "an impulse of noble desire which bears the soul irresistibly forward, as on the bosom of a swelling tide, toward the realization of the highest moral ends."[5]

[3]T. S. Eliot, "Murder in the Cathedral," *The Complete Poems and Plays* (New York: Harcourt, Brace and Co., 1950), p. 220.
[4]J. B. Mozley, *University Sermons* (New York: E. P. Dutton and Co., 1885), p. 340.
[5]J. C. Lambert, "Aspiration," *Encyclopedia of Religion and Ethics* (Edinburgh: T. and T. Clark, 1925), Vol. II, p. 127.

The term "aspiration" is primarily spiritual, having been born in the atmosphere of religion. It is closely related to spiritual ideals with which it maintains a reciprocal relationship. It is sometimes confused, however, with its second cousin called "ambition," which was born among the worldlings. Aspiration seeks spiritual values; ambition seeks sensate and worldly goals.

Aspiration is the motivation *par excellence*. It is superior to the voice of duty before which the human personality often becomes obstinate, confusing this voice with authoritarian figures against whom it is opposed unconsciously. Aspiration is superior to personal discipline which often breaks down through a lack of vigilance. It is superior to lofty resolutions which are frequently without inner motive power. "Let us learn to have noble desires," says Schiller, "and we shall have no need for sublime resolutions."

One can no more succeed in the spiritual life without spiritual aims and objectives than can a young man succeed in life without worthy objectives. Persons in all walks of life who have achieved success have envisioned challenging goals, while the drifters have been without definite aims. T. T. Munger says, "Providence has nothing good or high in store for one who does not resolutely aim at something good and high. A purpose is the eternal condition of success." Spiritual failure is usually the result of low aim, or of no aim.

Our secular culture makes it difficult for us today to have genuine spiritual aspirations. Personal success in today's world is equated primarily as proficiency in the market places. Our generation evaluates a man in terms of his income. We say that one man is a five-thousand-dollar-a-year man, and another, just twice as good, is a ten-thousand-dollar-a-year man. Our children grow up with this secular approach to values. When they come to adulthood they are usually low in spiritual aspirations for they too have observed that it is "exceedingly hard to put the spiritual life on a paying basis." Thus, being faithful to the training our culture gave them, they are tempted to make the secular things central and the spiritual things peripheral.

Modern man has a clear vision for secular goals, but dull vision for spiritual goals. It seems that some evil spirit, to use Kierkegaard's figure of speech, has put a pair of glasses on the nose of this generation. One of the lenses is a powerful magnifying glass; the other is an equally strong reducing glass.[6] Our generation looks at the secular things through the strong lens and at the spiritual things through the reducing one.

Worldly interests crowd out the interests of the spirit. The worldly things monopolize time and attention because they offer tangible and immediate sensory satisfactions. Modern man has lost much of his aspiration for the spiritual life through an indolence that has come from an indulgence in the sensate, like Kierkegaard's celebrated wild duck that lost his desire for flight because he grew fat and indolent through overeating in the farmyard.

The hope of every man in our generation is in the recovery and maintenance of spiritual aspirations. Life becomes one vast flatland without these, having no challenge to higher things. The spirit of immortal man becomes dull and sated when it occupies itself with trivia, like a brilliant boy in a slow-moving class. The boy spends his time in looking at the trivial things about him or in annoying subtly a fellow student. He does not know the reason for his boredom. Even more so, the immortal soul cannot be satisfied with only the sensate things of life since the soul was created for the Eternal.

There are those who have set out upon the spiritual quest because they have heard a call from the Beyond. They have seen that aspiration provides inspiration for life. They have found that their real self thrives in a zestful anticipation of spiritual values. They have responded affirmatively to Jesus'

[6]Soren Kierkegaard, *Either-Or* (Princeton: Princeton University Press, 1944), p. 20.

daring challenge: "But seek ye first the kingdom of God, and his righteousness. . . ." (Matthew 6:33). With Paul they give the things of the Spirit the highest priority. "Indeed I count everything as loss because of the surpassing worth of knowing Christ Jesus my Lord" (Philippians 3:8, R.S.V.). These people look beyond "the mass of follies and errors that make up so much of life." They have found that a genuine sense of spiritual values brings "a sabbath to the soul."

The wisdom literature of the Bible urges one to keep a healthful spiritual heart, to keep the dynamic center of attitudes and sentiments. "Keep thy heart with all diligence; for out of it are the issues of life" (Proverbs 4:23). Healthy spiritual attitudes are the dynamic for spiritual action in much the same way that the physical heart is the center of physical life.

Part III
Living Maturely

CHAPTER IX

Living in Secular Days

Secularism dominates the "psychological field" in which Christians live today. The field includes the Christian's total psychological environment, taking in everything to which he gives attention. Everything in the environment brings influence or pressure upon persons as they interact with it. Some of the factors in the psychological field have a high potency and others a low potency, like high and low pressure areas on a weather map. The high potency factors are often imbued with the secular spirit.

The man on the spiritual quest must recognize the nature of the contemporary secular spirit if he is to succeed in his Christian experience. He must know something of its view of life, and he needs to recognize that it inverts values. The contemporary Christian is like a man living in a strange and rigorous climate. He cannot protect himself against the hazards of it unless he has some knowledge of what to expect and for what to prepare.

Secularism means, most simply, a regard for the interests and affairs of this life to the neglect of matters pertaining to the future life. It represents the enthronement of personal interests and human sufficiency at the very center of life. Man takes a priority over God in the practical matters of life, and he maintains a nonchalant attitude toward Him. Some people "think God exists, some think not, some think it is impossible to tell, and the impression grows that it does

107

not matter."[1] The latter attitude is secular — a disposition to dispense with God in the give and take of life. In secularism, "temporal values are seen as ends in themselves," and men devote their lives to them.

The creative forces of Western civilization, indeed, of the whole world, for many decades have been secular. Emil Brunner "observes that the four men who have most profoundly influenced western thought in our time are Darwin, Nietzsche, Marx, and Freud."[2] The work of all of these men strengthened the secular forces of our age. Darwin complemented and augmented man's sense of self-sufficiency by suggesting that man had worked his way up from the brutes against terrific odds. Man was thus able to handle lesser problems, having demonstrated that he was fit to survive. Nietzsche glorified human wisdom and power in talking of supermen who had no need for God. Marx fostered secularism in a most radical form by decrying religion as an "opiate of the people." In sarcastic tones, he urged the multitudes to eat pie here on earth and not to wait for it in the sky. Freud strengthened the secular impulses by substituting psychoanalysis for religion. He said that religion was an illusion with no future. He would have men get "salvation," i.e., personal integration, on a psychoanalytic couch rather than on their knees before their Maker.

Secularism has invaded every area of modern life through the influence of these men, their disciples, and materialists of other kinds. Secularism is the dominant mood of the day. It pervades modern business where the profit motive dominates, even when thinly veiled by attitudes of service. It is prominent in education which often undertakes to train its students to be successful without reference to God. It permeates contemporary entertainment with its appeal to the senses. Scientism, with an arrogant intellectual imperialism,

[1]Walter Moberly, "The Crisis of a University," in *The Christian Century*, Oct. 8, 1958, p. 1142.
[2]Orlo Strunk, Jr., *Readings in Psychology of Religion* (New York: Abingdon Press, 1959), p. 246.

has arrogated to itself the authority to declare what is truth. Some scientists say that only that is true which can be taken into the laboratory, thus ruling out most religious convictions. The secular spirit has even invaded the realm of religion, and the church has become, in many instances, "a secularized version of the kingdom of God." People are religious because it is good for them. Religion gives them social status, and it helps them in their vocations.

Secularism is antithetical to the spiritual life. Jesus said that spiritual impulses are strangled because of an overconcern about earthly things. "And others are the ones sown among the thorns; they are those who hear the word, but the cares of the world, and the delight in riches, and the desire for other things, enter in and choke the word, and it proves unfruitful" (Mark 4:18, 19, R.S.V.). John warned his readers against secularism, asserting that it and the love of God were contrary.

> Do not love the world or the things in the world. If any one loves the world, love for the Father is not in him. For all that is in the world, the lust of the flesh and the lust of the eyes, and the pride of life, is not of the Father but is of the world (I John 2:15, 16, R.S.V.).

Paul recognized that it was the secular spirit that caused him to lose a one-time faithful companion. "For Demas, in love with this present world, has deserted me. . . ." (II Timothy 4:10, R.S.V.).

THE PSYCHOLOGY OF SECULARISM

There is a psychology of secularism as surely as there is a psychology of religion.[3] It has its own method of approach to the human personality; its own means of influencing human conduct. There are two elements in its methods.

[3]The term "psychology" is used here in an applied sense to suggest the application of psychological data to the study of secularism. Many psychologists, it should be noted, avoid such usages, preferring to employ the term only in a scientific sense.

First, it establishes a *selective perception* within persons. Second, secularism wastes away the *spiritual dynamics* of the human personality.

Secularism conditions the human personality to a type of selective perception in which sensate things are seen quickly and spiritual values are obscured. Jesus spoke clearly concerning this phenomenon. He said that the people in the thoughtless multitude, engulfed in the worldly affairs of life, heard His parables but perceived no truth in them. "So that they may indeed see but not perceive, and may indeed hear but not understand" (Mark 4:12, R.S.V.). He told the disciples that secular anxieties obscure truth. He said this after He observed that they were worried because they had forgotten to take food for a journey. "Having eyes, see ye not? and having ears, hear ye not? and do ye not remember?" (Mark 8:18) Their anxieties about temporal things had obscured the fact that the Christ who had fed the five thousand was with them.

The type of selective perception that conditions people against religious truths is called spiritual blindness in the Bible. This term represents the end result of weakened spiritual vision. Spiritual blindness is not a momentary unwillingness to look at the truth. It is rather the result of a debilitated religious life. Religious vision grows dim when the spiritual life atrophies as surely as physical vision grows dim when the optic nerve is damaged.

Spiritual perception is not a simple phenomenon; it is related to life broadly. It is rooted in a sense of spiritual need, in spiritual desires, and in an appreciation of truth. Secularism strikes at these sources of spiritual perception. It obscures the sense of needing divine help; it diminishes aspirations for spiritual values; and it lessens one's love of truth.

A sense of spiritual *need* is a basic condition of spiritual perception. A hungry man, for instance, is attentive to food, even looking for it, if necessary. A lonely man is attentive to people. A music lover is attentive to the kind of music he loves to hear.

Healthy spiritual *desires* are also a basic condition for religious perception. We tend to see the things that we want and to overlook other things. A little boy can see quickly a toy that he wishes even though it is surrounded by other merchandise in a show window. In adult life, we observe often that we hear readily the things we want to hear and that we are dull to those things that are undesirable.

Finally, an *appreciation of truth* is a condition for spiritual perception. Jesus said one must love the truth if he is to perceive it (Cf. John 3:10-21). Spiritual perception is dull if there is inhospitality to religious knowledge.

Spiritual truth is not available at the beck and call of a secularist who feels at times that he can make good use of religion. Arnold Toynbee says, "Remember, religion once lost, can never be whistled for, like a dog, to come back obediently, at man's convenience."

Every secularist is like Felix, who, busily engaged with the affairs of his province, sent Paul away after having heard an apostolic-sized sample of the Gospel. He said to Paul, "Go away for the present; when I have an opportunity I will summon you" (Acts 24:25b, R.S.V.). In the life of every man, unwanted spiritual truth departs, and with this truth out of sight, the secularist concentrates his attention on the sensate things about him.

Second, secularism weakens the spiritual dynamics of the human personality. It infects the interests with a worldly spirit, lowers the spiritual ideals, and weakens the religious attitudes. There is little drive toward the spiritual life when these basic motivating systems in human personality have been infected with the secular spirit.

Secularism has a tactical advantage over the spiritual view of life in appealing to human *interests* inasmuch as it always has its wares on display. They can be seen and handled. They are always near at hand and they can be possessed immediately, even on easy payment plans. Secularism has a strong appeal to practical-minded people, such as Americans, because secular values are utilitarian. We have been conditioned to appreciate gadgets more than ideas. In contrast to secularism, the spiritual life is intrinsic and its values are not displayed in a showcase. Spiritual life has a long perspective and it does not make all its worth immediately available. Moreover, it is costly, demanding full commitment of life, and its immediate utility is sometimes negative, actually diminishing some of the practical advantages in day to day living.

Secularism appeals to the human interests on the basis of ambition and sensory pleasure. This constitutes the essence of all temptation. "The essence of sin is putting self above God, guiding our own lives by our own standards. . . ."[4] Secularism constitutes the very atmosphere of sin because it wants God to leave man alone and let him do as he pleases.

This was the genius of Satan's temptation of Adam and Eve. The tempter overwhelmed our first parents with the glittering prospect: "Ye shall be as gods." The promised promotion appealed to them. Furthermore, Satan appealed to their sensory interests, "the tree was good for food, and that it was a delight to the eyes" (Genesis 3:6, R.S.V.).

A materialistic age, furthermore, weakens the spiritual dynamics of life by creating secular *ideals* for all to follow. In such an age the image of success is the image of a man who has won out in the business or professional world. His success is made graphic by the fact that he drives a car with ample chrome, belongs to an exclusive country club, and lives in a commodious house in the right section of town. Secularism is good to its faithful disciples and it honors them with recognition, seeing to it that their promotions are properly publicized in the press. It holds its faithful dis-

[4] Clifford E. Barbour, *Sin and the New Psychology* (New York: The Abingdon Press, 1930), p. 114.

ciples up as ideals for all ambitious and aspiring youth
to follow.

Hearty spiritual ideals are indispensable in the religious
life. Like mountain guides in the Alps, ideals are the guides
of those who undertake to climb the spiritual heights. To
be dependable in this matter, the ideals must be strong and
relatively free from secular impediments. They go on ahead,
giving challenge and direction to the spiritual climbers.
They call to them, saying, "Come on up, the view is more
expansive here and the atmosphere is more bracing."

Moreover, secularism wastes away the spiritual dynamics
by weakening the spiritual *attitudes* of personality. This
often happens in a subtle way without one's realizing what
is happening. One does not surrender primarily to the secular spirit by walking through a department store and looking
over the merchandise of a materialistic age. Spiritual attitudes are weakened, rather, in the give and take of interpersonal relationships. The attitudes of associates are con-
tagious. One catches the secular spirit through contact with
others, much as he catches the measles. Our secular associates create life situations that seem to demand surrender
to the spirit of the age. An overexpensive fur coat, for instance, never seemed important to a woman until her friend,
wife of a business associate of her husband, got one. The
coat then took on symbolic value. It became much more
than a wrap that would keep her warm. It stood for personal
status, assuring her that no unworthy personal comparison
could be made about her. Membership in a country club,
with accompanying expenditure of time, never seemed important to a businessman until his business peers joined.
Then life seemed to demand it lest he lack an important
item in the secular certification of success.

Insomuch as the psychological field is dominated by the
secular things, there is a mental and neural state of readiness
organized through experience to respond to the secular val-

ues and there is a state of unreadiness to respond to the spiritual things. In such a state a person is open, ready, and warm to the sensate things and callous, cold, and blind to religious things.

INVERTED VALUES

Secularism inverts the values of life. Jesus said, "But seek ye first the kingdom of God, and his righteousness; and all these things (the temporal necessities) shall be added to you" (Matthew 6:33). Secularism says to seek first the earthly and sensory things. It regards such matters as a spiritual kingdom and personal righteousness of dubious worth because they have no market value. The Christian needs to see this inversion of values.

In inverting the values of life, secularism has lowered the spiritual ideals and brought about a flatness to life. Secularism has no towering spiritual values, reaching toward heaven. It views life as one great plain of flatlands having neither depth nor height. Man moves along the earthly horizon for a period of seventy years, more or less, supplying his temporal needs, and then passes from the scene with no questions asked. During the time of his earthly existence, the secular man was too busy with the cares of life to explore the depth of his own spirit. Neither did he sense the pull of high ideals that comes from looking up to his Maker.

Secularism, in inverting life values, neglects the interests of the immortal spirit of man, assuming that this spirit can be satisfied with earthly things. It fails to see, with Hannah More, that, "the soul on earth is an immortal guest, compelled to starve at an unreal feast; a pilgrim panting for the rest to come; an exile anxious for its native home." The secular man fails to recognize that his soul is like the famished Bedouin, who, upon finding treasure in the desert, cried, "Alas, it is only diamonds." The secularist's condition is like that of the aestheticist, "rushing through life," as described by Kierkegaard. He is satiated and tires of everything, yet he hungers.[5]

The secularist misinterprets the nature of his hunger in believing that additional things can satisfy it. He is like the worldling whom God appropriately called, "Fool." This "egotistically ignorant man," as the original reference suggests, made the mistake of all secularists in assuming that spiritual needs could be satisfied by earthly goods. In great prosperity he said with dramatic flourish, "Soul, you have ample goods laid up for many years; take your ease, eat, drink, be merry" (Luke 12:19b, R.S.V.).

The secularist substitutes earthly prosperity for spiritual welfare. He says, in the words of the Church in Laodicea: "I am rich, I have prospered, and I need nothing" (Revelation 3:17a, R.S.V.). He says this in spiritual blindness, not knowing that really he is "wretched, pitiable, poor, blind, and naked" (Revelation 3:17b, R.S.V.).

Secularism misinterprets the way to obtain the basic and enduring values of life. The secularist undertakes to satisfy his profound wish for personal security by amassing possessions rather than by having faith in his Heavenly Father. He tries to satisfy his wish for God's approval by the approval of his fellowmen; his wish for divine acceptance by the acceptance of a religious institution. He sometimes seeks inner peace by free association with a psychiatrist instead of confession to God. He tries to buy joy for his hours of leisure, forgetting that true joy is never a marketable commodity but is always an achievement of the human spirit or the gift of God.

The secularist misinterprets the nature of religion. He sometimes regards it as a useful means, sort of a short cut, that will help him get the things that he wants. He thus undertakes to use religious resources in a type of spiritual exploitation. He engages in corporate worship because it

[5]Soren Kierkegaard, *Either — Or* (Princeton: Princeton University Press, 1944), p. 20.

is relaxing and it gives him renewed energy for another week of competitive endeavor. Moreover, useful insights sometimes come while the choir sings and occasionally the minister suggests an idea that is useful in dealing with people. He engages in the sacraments with a utilitarian attitude, regarding the Lord's supper as a type of magic that quite automatically rights things with God, without a deep personal commitment to Him and without a faithful identification with His purposes. He uses prayer as a labor saver; or, as a means of getting out of difficult life situations. Secularists read their Bibles with the same kind of bargain-minded attitude. Daniel Defoe once wrote of his characters, "When these characters get into a tight place, they hastily thumb through their Bibles. But it is not their peace that they want to make with God; it is a bargain." The secularist thinks of faith as confidence in self, in one's fellowmen, in democratic institutions, and in the laws of our economy.

The Christian faith is characterized by its long-time perspective in contrast to the secular view of life. It believes that man is "over-built for this world." The Christian seeks to "live in two worlds," the temporal and the spiritual.

The practicing Christian meets the demands of his immortal spirit by providing it with both a good retrospect and a good prospect. The Christian can look over his past life with a sense of humility and know that he has lived for things that endure. Like Abraham, he has sought a city whose builder and maker was God (Hebrews 11:10).

The retrospect of the secularist is not like that. Many people spend their declining years in disillusionment, feeling that life has been characterized by minus instead of plus signs. Their last years are spent in secret penance for they sense that an irreparable mistake was made in their neglect of their immortal souls. They find it hard to change in their evening years because life has acquired so much momentum that it is difficult to alter its direction.

The prospect of the secularist in his later years is characterized by a sense of emptiness and futility. He has experienced all the adventures of life. He looks forward with no steadfast hope. With Solomon, as a disillusioned old man, he says, "Vanity of vanities, all is vanity."

The prospect of the Christian is promising. He believes that the future belongs to those who prepare for it. There is always a better "tomorrow" for him, even in old age. He always faces the sunrise of a new and better day. He never has occasion to say with an actor dying at forty years of age, "Pull down the curtain, the farce is over." Instead, even in old age, he says, "Lift the curtain; new life is ahead."

CHAPTER X

Developing Faith Capacity

The faith capacity of Christians differs greatly. The differences in this area of Christian personality are greater than differences in height, weight, and physical appearance. Our faith quotients differ more than our intelligence quotients.

We are using the term "faith" in this chapter to suggest a trusting attitude in God. It is a specific confidence that He, as Heavenly Father, will provide the things that His children need.

Faith is the vital principle, the *elan vital,* of the Christian. It supplies the needs of the spiritual life, something like the blood stream provides for the interior physical needs. Faith is indispensable in Christian living. Let it cease and spiritual life ceases; let it grow weak and spiritual life becomes enfeebled. Let it be strong and spiritual life is strong.

CONDITIONING FACTORS OF FAITH

Numerous factors in life bring about a conditioning of the ability to believe. Some of these factors are internal and others are external; some of them help faith and others hinder it. Insight into the conditioning factors is essential to growth in the matter of trusting God. Self-knowledge and growth in faith are intrinsically related. There are five conditioning factors that are important in this matter.

1. *Inborn temperamental tendencies affect one's faith ability.* The person born with a tendency to be joyous, the sanguine type of personality, has a disposition to look favor-

ably toward all of life and he finds it easy to trust a Heavenly Father whom he believes is benevolent. On the other hand, the melancholic person has temperamental factors that limit his faith. With a tendency to concentrate attention on his troubles, he finds it difficult to trust God.

Basic attitudes toward life, often rooted in temperament, have a strong influence on one's ability to trust God. Positive attitudes toward self and life help one to reach out for the blessings one believes that God has provided for His children, while negativistic attitudes bring about an unconscious hesitancy about God's actual willingness to give good things to those who ask Him. A healthy self-confident attitude helps one to reach by faith for something better, while the overly submissive attitude leads one to "submit," believing that God has nothing better for him. The progressive attitude toward life helps to prepare one to believe that God will help him to advance to new levels, while the overly conservative attitude suggests that he should hold on to the values that he has and not risk their loss in an adventure for new things.

2. *Past personal experiences relate to faith ability.* Faith is learned in human situations. The homes in which we were reared, the schools and churches that we attended, and the friends we made, all served to advance or retard the development of our faith capacity. We learned to trust or mistrust God in learning to trust or mistrust our fellowmen, His children created in His image.

Favorable experiences with people, especially in early life, are important in the development of faith in God. The adult who lived as a child in a home in which all the members of the family contributed wholesomely to the welfare of the others, was reared in a psychological and spiritual climate favorable to the development of faith. In such a family, we may assume, parental promises were kept, and the father and mother responded discreetly to the requests of the children. The situation was still more favorable if the parents supplemented their own examples of concern for the family by teaching the child that God also provided wisely and generously for His children.

One's own past experiments in faith also condition his ability to trust God. Forgotten experiences of successful faith give one an unconscious predisposition to trust God again. On the other hand, repressed experiences of failure in faith bring about an unconscious hesitancy to believe.

3. *Faith depends heavily on personal adjustment.* Maladjusted persons usually have little capacity to trust. The person with a deep sense of inadequacy and inferiority, for instance, seldom has great faith. He projects his personal inferiorities onto God. There is a positive relationship between a healthful sense of self-esteem and faith. The man who lacks a proper confidence in himself will likely lack confidence in God, his Maker.

The anxiety-ridden person finds it hard to trust God. Free floating anxiety spreads nebulous doubts through the whole personality. Hidden fears, as phantom anxieties hiding in the secrecy of repression, hinder one's ability to trust God. Anxious fear and confident faith are in a dynamic opposition to each other.

Guilt feelings restrict the ability to trust. There is often a great increase in faith capacity when actual guilt is forgiven. However, a morbid sense of guilt sometimes remains after that forgiveness. This sense of guilt is based usually in tendencies toward neuroticism. Such morbid guilt feelings obscure the face of God and immobilize faith through an extravagant sense of self-condemnation. Persons with a morbid sense of guilt feel estranged from God. Feelings of estrangement are incompatible with faith. One does not trust strangers in the same manner one trusts friends.

Masochism is perhaps the most crucial maladjustment that affects faith. Masochism is an unconscious desire to be punished or to suffer. This impulse is sometimes demonstrated by criminals who leave behind unmistakable evidence that will lead to their arrest.

The masochistic person unconsciously does not want to believe. He spurns God's offered blessings, choosing rather a way of inner suffering. He inflicts a type of religious torture on himself in which he takes a morbid pleasure, feeling that his suffering will ultimately win God's eternal mercy. He undertakes to say to God, as it were, "Do you see how much I have suffered; won't that make up for my sins?"

The masochistic impulse is crucial at the point of a sense of divine forgiveness. The person who has an unconscious motive to suffer, perhaps rooted in a morbid sense of guilt, finds it hard to be justified by faith. He confesses his sins, apparently commits himself to God, yet he is unable to accept divine pardon. He has a deep-seated motive to suffer for his sins. In many cases, he cannot forgive himself so he finds it hard to believe that God will forgive him. He is loaded with feelings of neurotic unworthiness. Even after the conversion of such a man, he may again become guilt-ridden because he inwardly wishes to carry a load of sin.

4. *Faith also depends on one's view of the universe.* The man who believes that God is the Maker of all things, including the laws of the universe, has a good basis for faith. He thinks of the world as God's workshop and he senses the nearness of the Divine. On the contrary, the man who conceives of the world as being in the grip of an impersonal hand has little basis for an active faith in God.

Numerous assumptions of science have done man a disservice in developing faith. In their preoccupation with sensory things, scientists, like secularists, have sometimes assumed, and actually said, that God does not exist. More frequently, however, and just as destructively, they have assumed that His existence did not matter. As with Deists, they have thought that whatever God there might be was an absentee landlord who gave no concern to the world He made. The positivistic approach of science has suggested to some people that the only real and dependable things are those that can be weighed and measured. This attitude leads to a distrust of the unseen realities. It is hard to develop trust in a personal God in a mentality of scientific positivism.

A vital faith demands a sensitivity of God's immanent presence which becomes a warm climate for the development of the trusting attitude. The sense of His presence gives a "reality feeling" to spiritual objectives and values. It stimulates a spiritual imagination and fosters spiritual perception as to what God desires to do for His children. It makes the spiritual things a "live option" among the transient things of the world. It gives the heart courage to move forward in venturesome action.

5. *Faith depends, finally, on right moral and spiritual intentions.* Cooperation with God in the moral laws of the universe brings a sense of identity with divine purposes which strengthens faith. Also, vision is clear when one faces the right. The shadows fall back of those who walk toward the light.

A life of faith is impossible when one is estranged from God through evil-doing and impenitence. A lack of sincere moral intention undercuts the basis for faith. When a jaunty skeptic admitted his grave doubts about the Trinity, a man of simple faith rightly answered, "But aren't you weak also on the Ten Commandments?" The heart is more important in developing faith capacity than is the head; morals are more important than deductive reasoning. Sincere spiritual intention and faith are inextricably united: "If ye abide in me, and my words abide in you, ye shall ask what ye will, and it shall be done unto you" (John 15:7). The New Testament word for faith assumes a spiritual basis. It signifies "obedience-in-trust."

A CURRICULUM FOR BUILDING FAITH

Jesus accepted His disciples as men of "little faith" and, as a master teacher, He introduced them into a psychological-spiritual curriculum of faith-building that demonstrated His superb knowledge of human nature. He proceeded on psychologically valid principles. There were two prominent elements in His course of study. He emphasized acquaintance with God — the object of their belief; and He provided for supervised practice in the development of faith.

Acquaintance With the Divine Develops Faith Capacity. Jesus selected twelve disciples that "they should be with him, and that he might send them forth to preach, And to have power to heal sicknesses, and to cast out devils" (Mark 3:14b, 15). The association of the disciples with Jesus brought them to know Him and God the Father. In knowing God the disciples knew the object of their faith. No man will trust God if he does not know Him.

Faith is based on personal acquaintance in both human and divine relationships. Faith in our fellow men, for example, is based on a personal knowledge of them. We do not usually trust strangers though they may represent high qualities of integrity. We have confidence in our proven friends because we are acquainted with their attitudes, ideals, and habits. We have seen our friends in action, demonstrating the principles of integrity in their behavior.

One evening a stranger went to a midweek prayer meeting at a church in which he knew no one. During the meeting, this man, being a Christian, participated in the services by offering a voluntary prayer and later by testifying that he was a Christian. After the benediction, however, he, having lost his billfold during the day, asked one of the men for a small loan. The man, in spite of the prayer and testimony, declined explaining in a half truth that he too "was a little short" just then.

The stranger had come to that town in prospect of a job,

and upon getting it, moved his family there. They all attended that church and became acquainted with the people. A year later, the man asked again for a loan, following a prayer service. This time the response was otherwise. The one who had formerly declined, pulled out his billfold and made a generous and gracious loan. How do you account for the change in attitude? The same man had made the same request. Acquaintanceship is the reason. We trust our proven friends.

It is much like that in developing confidence in God. J. M. Coleman, one-time teacher in Greenville College, used to ask his classes dramatically, "Why don't men trust God?" His answer was succinct and comprehensive, "Because they do not know Him." Men doubt that God is willing to help them because they are not acquainted with Him. They do not really believe in His integrity because they do not know Him.

There are two primary ways by which men become acquainted with God. First, they learn to know Him through the study of the Bible and other religious literature. Second, they learn to know Him through worship.

1. *Paul stated that faith is increased by an acquaintance with God through a knowledge of the Scriptures.* "Faith cometh by hearing, and hearing by the word of God" (Romans 10:17). John said that he wrote the gospel that bears his name so as to increase the faith of his readers. "But these are written, that ye might believe that Jesus is the Christ, the Son of God; and that believing ye might have life in his name" (John 20:31). John saw Jesus' work as the expression of the will of God. He was the living Word of God, very God in action. Thus, one knew God the Father in knowing Jesus Christ.

Many of the words in the Bible are self-authenticating and they inspire faith within the reader. Jesus' portrayal of

God's concern for His creation, including the birds of the air and the lilies of the field, kindles an attitude in the reader to trust God even in the little things of daily life. The confidently reported miracles of healing, unaffected by arguments for their authenticity, assure the reader that God cares about man's physical need. The account of the feeding of the five thousand inspires confidence that God can supply our every temporal need. The forthright statements that even the nations are in God's hands build faith for crucial days.

2. Moreover, *faith is increased by acquaintance with God through worship*. Both public and private prayer is communion with God. It is more than a monologue, more than a soliloquy in which an orphaned man talks to himself. It is more than a busily occupied person sending telegrams, perhaps night letters, to heaven. Genuine prayer is like a telephone conversation. There is a divine response in true prayer.

In His response, God communicates a sense of His presence which sets fire to one's knowledge of theological matters. The sense of His presence gives a new reality feeling about His existence. It brings an intuitive certitude about His concern for His creatures. It personalizes one's theology because of the sense of an I-Thou relationship. It underwrites the promises of God with an inner sense of certainty. It makes faith seem like a natural and dependable activity of life.

Practice in Believing Develops Faith Capacity. Jesus recognized the validity of the principle that one learns by doing. He thus supervised the practice of faith in His disciples. He sent them out on tours into communities that were filled with raw human needs. "Heal the sick, cleanse the lepers, raise the dead, cast out devils" (Matthew 10:8a). Jesus gave the disciples basic instructions before they went out on their mission and He evaluated the results upon their return.

The disciples learned faith both by their successes and by their failures. Every success was a personal confirmation that God would honor their faith. Their failures called for times of re-examination and instruction. Upon failing to cast out the demon in a demon-possessed boy, the disciples asked Jesus, "Why could not we cast him out?" (Matthew 17:19). Moreover, their failure also emphasized their need for more faith and they prayed, "Lord, increase our faith" (Luke 17:5b).

Men today learn faith by practice in believing as surely as did the disciples. Faith is a skill, an art, and one can no more achieve it by reading a book than one can learn to play a piano by reading music theory. The practice of faith, however, needs to be under guidance, as do experiments in a college laboratory. Experimentation without supervision usually becomes a waste of time in a futile exercise of trial and error. The Holy Spirit directs the learner of faith in believing.

George Mueller learned faith by believing. He started to pray for small donations for his orphanage, and as his prayers were answered he increased the size of his requests. Finally, he reported, he could ask for ten thousand dollars as readily as he asked for the first ten dollars. A law of increased returns operates in faith. Every answer to prayer increases one's believing capacity.

No man can by-pass the practical aspect in the curriculum of faith. Faith is only theory to the man who does not practice it. Like honor, one cannot believe in it until he practices it. Academic faith, i.e., a theory about faith, is worth little in itself. God wishes every Christian to build up a body of empirical data proving that He answers his prayers.

The development of faith capacity offers man his greatest challenge in the area of personal growth. No personal achievement will accomplish more than a living trust in God. Faith is a different kind of approach to problems. It represents a divine-human cooperation to all kinds of problems, both great and small. Faith offers contemporary man an opportunity to obtain divine wisdom for human ignorance, divine guidance for human lostness. Faith offers God's poise for man's sense of insecurity, and God's power for man's inadequacy.

CHAPTER XI

Perceiving God's Guidance

Divine guidance is not given to persons indiscriminately. It is not like the rain that falls on the just and unjust. Guidance is granted to those who seek it. It comes to those who are prepared to receive it. There is an earned right in receiving heavenly direction. There are basic psychological-spiritual principles that must be followed if one is to receive a personal knowledge of God's will. In the first place, one must maintain spiritual-psychological attitudes that open the mind to a knowledge of the divine will. Secondly, one must use tested methods through which God makes His guidance known.

Maintaining Receptive Attitudes

1. *A sense of dependence on God is basic to a personal knowledge of His will.* The "sense of absolute dependence" is important, indeed, to the whole Christian life, as Friedrich Schleiermacher emphasized, but it has unique significance in the matter of divine guidance. The self-sufficient man does not "trouble" God with his problems. He believes he can solve them himself. The person with a "superiority complex" has a closed mind to the reception of God's will. He already has all the answers to his questions. On the other hand, a healthful sense of dependence on God provides motivation in the quest for heavenly guidance. The man who relies on God is like a young scholar who recog-

nizes the limitations of his knowledge. He knows there are vast areas awaiting intellectual exploration in his chosen field of study and he pursues his search with humility and zeal.

The circumstances of human life are such that all of us may well feel a sense of dependence on God. It is normal for us to feel that we are amateurs in the art of effective living. If any one of us ever came to the place where we felt we were a "professional" in the art of living we soon met a difficult life situation that reduced us again to the amateur status.

Young people normally feel that they are amateurs in life. They confront new personal experiences and they must answer some of life's most basic questions. A young person chooses, for instance, a life vocation and life companion in his early adult career.

Middle-aged people normally feel that they are amateurs in the art of living as they seek to solve the problems in personal religion, community, vocation, and family. For instance, few parents feel like professionals in the matter of rearing their families. They are often nonplussed by the unique problems that arise. Rather than boasting of their competence, they are likely to say, "We are in the process of learning to bring up our children inasmuch as this is the first family that we ever had."

Persons in later maturity normally feel like amateurs in life as they seek to make the difficult adjustments of older age. They know the difficulty of adjusting to retirement in a manner that will save their last days from a sense of futile monotony. They also know that there are difficult problems related to the adjustment to reduced income, diminished strength, and curtailed activity. Many older people believe that they entered the last period of life poorly prepared to meet its problems, more poorly prepared than they entered any other period.

2. *Every man who seeks divine guidance must maintain a positive attitude toward God's will.* He must consider a knowledge of the divine will for him as one of the great constructive forces of life. There is often a real problem at this very point. There are those who regard God's will in a negative manner. Secretly they wish to avoid it. They unconsciously feel that God's commands are rooted in the prohibitions of life. They have been conditioned to believe that His ways constrict life rather than expand it. Such negative attitudes make it difficult to sense God's leadership.

The New Testament concept of God's will is not rooted in negative and arbitrary decrees of the Almighty but in His fatherly desires and wishes for His children. Both of the basic Greek words for God's *will* in the New Testament have the elements of desire and wish in them. In many cases they can be translated "the *desires* of God," or "the *wishes* of God." Divine guidance is rooted in a great fatherly love that gives origin to benevolent wishes for His children. Henry Drummond said, "God never unnecessarily thwarts a man's nature and his liking. It is a mistake to think that His will is always in line with the disagreeable."

On the other hand, a realistic attitude recognizes that God does not pamper His children. The ultimate good is not always the most pleasant. The writer of the epistle to the Hebrews has a relevant word of wisdom on this matter. He says that God often chastens His children because He loves them. Discipline has an important place in divine-human relationships, as it has in the rearing of children (Hebrews 12:3-11).

The ability to view God and His guidance in an objective manner depends heavily on a healthy balance of the permissive and prohibitive aspects of early environment. The man who was reared in an overly rigid and prohibitive home often has a tendency to feel that God usually says "No" to the requests of His children. He views God as an overly rigid cosmic parent who takes a secret delight in prohibitions. On the other hand, the pampered child, brought up in an overly permissive home, often expects God to pamper him. He has little ability to hear the Almighty say "No" to his requests. He really views God as a great, indulgent and easygoing father who cares little what His darling children do, just so long as they have a good time.

3. *Willingness to follow God's will is essential to a knowledge of it.* "If any man will do his will, he shall know of the doctrine . . ." (John 7:17). Henry Drummond said that 90 per cent of the difficulty in knowing God's will is in a lack of commitment to Him. The disposition of the heart is more important in this matter than the reasoning powers of the mind. God does not normally reveal His will to man if the man is set to resist it. Much ignorance in this area is self-chosen ignorance. We do not know because we do not want to know.

There is a vast difference in the conditions for a knowledge of nature and for a knowledge of God's will for us.

> Nature is indifferent to the moral character of the scientist, except in the one vital point of intellectual integrity. Nature will reveal her secrets equally to saint and scoundrel if each knows how to put the right questions. But in the knowledge of divine things the whole man is involved: intellect and conduct, thought and trust, knowledge and the desires of the heart. What you know depends on what kind of a man you are. Only the pure in heart shall see God.[1]

A lack of willingness to do God's will narrows one's field of spiritual perception. It brings about selective perception. One sees and hears what he wants to see and hear. "There is no one so deaf as he who does not wish to hear." The person who is unwilling to do God's will has a closed mental

[1]*Interpreter's Bible* (Nashville: The Abingdon Press, 1955), Vol. XI, p. 608.

circuit on his hearing, as the child who pays little attention to what is said to him until he hears something mentioned that he wishes to do.

Willingness to do God's will, as a condition of divine guidance, needs to be demonstrated in the small things of life. Henry Drummond said that the "doing of God's will in the small things is the best preparation for doing it in the great things." This is the real training ground for developing a receptive attitude toward God. "A man ought not to expect light on God's will in life's intricacies of conduct if he is unwilling to follow a clear will in life's simplicities."

4. *The seeker after divine guidance must make full use of his mental powers.* Man cannot expect God to do his homework for him, as an overly indulgent father. He must expect to apply the principles of reason to the problems of life as a competent student applies himself to the problems of mathematics. God is too wise to pamper His children by giving them the answers which they can obtain themselves. The Heavenly Father takes no delight in speaking to thoughtless minds. Even divine thoughts like to associate with human ideas.

Paul emphasizes the principle of thoughtfulness in Ephesians. "Wherefore be ye not unwise, but understanding what the will of the Lord is" (Ephesians 5:17). The word translated "unwise" literally means "mindless," or, in stronger words, "stupid." The Greek word translated "understanding" means literally, "to put together, to compound, or to synthesize." Paul wanted the Ephesian Christians to see the meaning of things in their inner relationships. He urged them to bring all their mental ability to the task of discovering God's will. He expected them to carry on a thoughtful examination of the facts that related to their situation and form them into a whole.

There are four relevant elements in the human method

of solving problems. These elements have a wide usage and they are especially applicable to the practical problems of life.

1. Look at all the facts that relate to the problem. Insight depends upon a comprehensive view of the situation.
2. Relax after you have viewed the situation broadly. In doing this your unconscious will give you perspective.
3. Receive insight. This often comes while the unconscious forces of your mind relate the pertinent elements.
4. Verify the insight. In the Christian life this may be done by corroborating evidence obtained by reason, from the Bible, by prayer, and from the counsel of trusted friends.

It must be recognized, moreover, that the solution to many of life's problems surpasses human ability. It is then that the thoughtful person turns to the Holy Spirit for special direction. Like a master teacher, the Spirit illuminates the obscure parts of the equation and leads one to the right answer.

USING APPROVED METHODS

1. *The Bible, as the Christian's textbook, is a source of divine guidance.* It is filled with divine light on human life. The Psalmist said that the Scriptures were as "a lamp unto my feet, and a light unto my path" (Psalm 119:105). He found his Scriptures so lifelike that he personified them, saying that they were "my counsellors" (Psalm 119:24). He discovered in actual experience that the entrance of God's Word "giveth light, it giveth understanding unto the simple" (Psalm 119:130).

The Bible provides light on life by presenting vivid reports of living dramas of actual men and women who were seeking God's will. It tells about divine guidance in the common life as it relates the unaffected story of Abraham's servant being guided by God as he searched for a wife for Isaac (Genesis 24:1-67). It reports divine guidance in national crises as in the vivid account of King Hezekiah seeking direction as he spread before God the threatening letter from an arrogant enemy (Isaiah 37:14-20). In strongly moving language, it tells of how Jesus Himself sought the Father's will in the Garden of Gethsemane (Matthew 26:36-46).

The Bible sets forth God's will for man in its history, biographies, commandments, sermons, parables, and all its other types of literature. This enduring revelation of the divine mind on the problems of human experience constitutes a standard by which every man may evaluate his hypotheses about life problems. Thus, the Christian, like the scientist, can critically evaluate contemporary theories about life in the light of settled principles.

The Bible offers the clearest guidance to those who know it best. A law of increasing returns operates here. The Bible brings much to the man who brings much to it. It offers least to the one who grasps it up in the hope of getting a guiding word hurriedly.

Guidance comes to the man who maintains a receptive attitude toward the Scriptures. The receptive attitude is as important as the searching attitude. The one seeking guidance needs to read the Bible with "an eager mind, purified by rigorous religious discipline, relaxed yet alert, expectantly open to the most delicate suggestions of the most High." The biblical materials speak to a person with such an attitude. The reading of the story of a depressed Elijah brings courage and guidance to the discouraged. The story of a guilt-ridden David points the way of release to the man with an oppressive sense of sin. The account of Peter's fear and anxiety on the night of Jesus' betrayal becomes a counselor to the person in like circumstances. The record of Paul's steadfast purpose amid trials and tribulations gives guidance and stamina to the hardpressed Christian.

2. *Prayer is another means of obtaining divine guidance.*
It provides man an opportunity to get insight on life problems, by the help of the Holy Spirit, as he outlines his need
to God in a counselor-counselee situation. A sense of the
divine presence in times of prayer helps to create this kind
of situation. A sense of divine acceptance enables a man to
express freely every aspect of his problem, even the negative
elements. Also, audible praying assists in making the situation more objective and lifelike. Insight often comes as a
person prays outlining every relevant aspect of his situation
to God. In such praying, the Almighty is a good listener,
like effective human counselors.

The Christian prepares the way for the reception of divine
guidance in prayer by clearing away spiritual obstructions.
He opens his mind to the divine wisdom when he acknowledges sincerely that he is unable to solve his problems. Self-
dependence gives way to God-dependence. He prepares
his mind for a grasp of the eternal values when he recognizes
the temporal nature of secular things. He lessens the clamor
of emotions for immediate pleasures as he prayerfully seeks
an eternal perspective. The long view of life causes the
primary things of life to come into prominence and the
secondary things to retreat. Prayer has cleansing power,
comparable to psychological catharsis, when one acknowledges his self-will. Prayer diminishes the power of wishful
thinking as one fearlessly recognizes the existence of such
thinking. In hours of the right kind of praying, issues are
clarified, divine guidance is received, decisions are made,
and one goes forth with inner strength to carry out God's will.

3. *Counseling provides another means of obtaining a
personal knowledge of God's will.* The values of a full discussion of a difficult life situation with a trusted confidant
are great. The confidant may be a wise friend, a Christian
minister, or a trained therapist.

A Christian counselor helps one find God's will for his life in a number of ways. Frequently, he helps by motivating one's thinking by the use of relevant questions. At other times, he offers thoughtful suggestions that open new areas for exploration. Furthermore, his own objectivity about one's situation often alerts one to the highly subjective elements in his thinking. At times, the wise counselor speaks a self-authenticated word of wisdom which the mind of the counselor immediately confirms. At other times his well-timed assurances keep the counselee searching for God's answer when he might have given up because of frustration.

There are times when the counselor provides the most assistance by being a good listener. This gives the counselee an opportunity to talk freely about his situation in an atmosphere of acceptance. The sincere concern of the counselor constitutes a good spiritual-psychological climate for insight.

One contemporary college teacher and counselor recently gave an example of the value of good listening. A college boy had come to her for counsel. He started to relate his difficulty but after saying a few words he became emotional and began to speak in a low voice. The counselor asked the boy to repeat what he had said and to speak more loudly. He began again but after a few words he was inarticulate. The counselor then explained that her hearing was poor and she urged the young man to speak loudly and clearly. The student started his story again but soon his voice dropped. The counselor did not ask the youth to start over but she sat attentively while feigning comprehension. Upon finishing his story the young man arose and thanked his teacher for solving his problem for him. When relating this incident several months later the counselor said that she had not learned at the time nor later what was the young man's problem. However, she had, in a real sense, solved his problem by good "listening." She had created a situation in which the counselee saw the answer as he viewed his problem in the presence of a concerned person.

4. *The interpretation of God's providential acts consti-tutes a fourth means of divine guidance.* This is guidance by circumstances. In following this method, one assumes that favorable circumstances indicate God's leadership along those lines and that unfavorable circumstances indicates His forbiddance. Sometimes God is said to lead by opening and closing doors as He did with Paul and Silas. He closed the door for them to preach in Asia Minor because He wanted them to enter Europe.

Guidance by circumstances is an important but difficult means whereby one may discern God's will. Victor Hugo says, "God makes visible to men his will in events, an obscure text written in a mysterious language." It takes a sound head, an honest heart, and a humble spirit to discern God's will in the providences of life.

This is an auxiliary method of guidance. Every open door must be examined in the light of other methods. If this is not done one will spend his life wandering about through open doors with no clear sense of direction. On the other hand, this method is useful in confirming guidance received by other means.

Guidance by circumstances is valuable to those who have fully committed their ways to God. They are thus willing to walk through open doors though they lead to paths of sacrifice. Sometimes, for example, they feel that God is lead-ing them along a certain line but they find a closed door blocking their way. If that door opens to them in response to their faith it is a strong confirmation to them that God is leading.

Divine guidance brings about confident living. Kipling remarks in one of his Indian stories that "there is only one thing more terrible in battle than a regiment of desperadoes officered by a half dozen young dare-devils, and that is a company of Scotch Presbyterians who rise from their knees and go into action convinced that they are about to do the will of God." Man moves forward in his spiritual quest with strength when he believes he is in God's will.

CHAPTER XII

Demonstrating Dynamic Christian Love

There are two general attitudes toward Christ among those who profess His name. One attitude is rooted in admiration of Him; the other is seen in a deep personal loyalty to Him. The attitude of admiration is primarily emotional and sentimental; the attitude of loyalty is rooted in esteem and reverence. Admiration represents a type of superficial love; loyalty arises out of a profound love. Admiration is human; Christian love has large divine elements. Admiration is static; Christian love is dynamic. The latter serves as the motivating center of the Christian life.

ADMIRERS OF CHRIST

Kierkegaard contrasts "admirers" of Christ and "followers" of Him. Many professed Christians, he said, substitute religious admiration for discipleship. The mere admirer is indisposed to sacrifice personally for Christ and he is unwilling to reconstruct his life to become what he admires. He makes his religion a matter of "words, verbal expressions, asseverations (and) he is inexhaustible in affirming how highly he prizes Christianity."[1] The follower, on the other hand, "aspires to be what he admires." The sincere follower is in agreement with the Cambridge Platonists who said that Christianity is "a way of walking, not a way of talking."

[1]Soren Kierkegaard, *Training in Christianity* (Princeton: Princeton University Press, 1941), p. 245.

The admirer looks upon Christ with great delight, rejoicing in the beauty of His character. He sings Christian hymns with enthusiasm and he is inspired by literature and art that relate to Christ. He often has high ideals and he appreciates righteousness both in person and in society. He looks forward to the spread of the kingdom of God and he rejoices in every advance of the church. The admirers have kindly feelings about Christ. They have a "tear of elegant sentiment" in their eyes permanently for their faith.

Kierkegaard says that those who are only admirers of Christ "poetize" the Christian faith. They commit the sin of "poetizing instead of being." They stand in relationship to Christianity only through imagination. The Danish philosopher compared Christians of his day to the man who became unhappy in love and therefore became a poet blissfully extolling the happiness of love.[2] This tendency to live in the imagination brought about a condition in nineteenth-century Christianity in Denmark, and elsewhere, which was described as "diluted, enervated sentimentality and refined Epicureanism." Religious admirers are romanticists about their faith. They center their religion in their emotions. They like "to play on the sentimental flute" of religion.

James Boswell, biographer of Samuel Johnson, is an example of a man who sought to unite religious sentiment with a worldly delight in sinful pleasures. He was "addicted to the most eloquent repentance and at the same time to explanations that the sins of which he repents were not, after all, serious."[3] Boswell considered himself a staunch friend of religion yet he yielded to every temptation. He was a bundle of contradictions and he delighted both in piety and in sin. "He chuckled amid his pious groans," writes Robert Lynd. Moreover, Lynd compared him to a man married to

[2]Soren Kiekegaard, *The Sickness Unto Death* (Princeton: Princeton University Press, 1941), pp. 123-126.
[3]Robert Lynd, *Dr. Johnson and Company* (Garden City: Doubleday, Doran and Co., 1928), p. 47.

both virtue and vice and who enjoys playing the one of them against the other. Perhaps Boswell was not totally a deliberate hypocrite. He had developed the ability to make a cheap sentimental substitute for right living.

The kindly feelings of the mere admirers of Christ are due largely to their social inheritance. They learned their religion as they learned to appreciate worth and beauty in other parts of their culture. They have sentimental feelings about their religious faith because their family had them. Theirs is an inherited religion. They are children of Christians and not Christians themselves. They have never had a personal confrontation with Christ that involved personal repentance and a living faith.

Those who admire Christ but do not follow Him make easygoing assumptions about the value of admiration in Christian experience. They uncritically assume that respect for Christ and for Christian ideals makes them Christian. They fail to see that Christ's call involves a call to action; that Christian discipleship means obedience to the Master. These people permit many of their moral impulses "to remain in the soft haze of Christian sentiment." They have never grasped the concept, expressed by James Russell Lowell, "that all the beautiful sentiments in the world weigh less than a single lovely action." The Christian sentimentalists desire to have "the luxury of an emotion without praying for it." They have forgotten that Jesus rejected a group of "admirers" with incisive words, "And why call ye me Lord, Lord, and do not the things which I say?" (Luke 6:46).

Those who only admire Christ are filled with ambivalence. Their minds are full of mixed feelings about the Christian faith. They are ambivalent about sin. They sorrow over their sins "aesthetically" but they do not forsake them. Much of their repentance is verbal. They renounce sin in holy precincts but they embrace it in everyday life. They are both idealists and realists, and their Christian idealism is often compromised in the face of their worldly realism. Milton referred to this class of people in saying, "Most men admire virtue, who follow not her love." Kierkegaard said that many philosophers build mansions of moral theory while they themselves live in nearby ethical shacks. "Admirers" in the Christian faith see only one side of the character of Christ. They do not view Him as a spiritual revolutionary because they themselves "have an infinite dread of everything radical."

The total religious experience of "admirers" of Christ is ambivalent. Christ is not really central in their lives because there are other interests struggling for dominance. Religion is indeed important to them but there are some equally important interests. There are joys in Christian living but there are competitive joys in earthly pursuits. There is a commitment to Christ but with a limited sense of abandonment. In the lives of such Christians there is little audacity of faith and little Christian adventure because their religion is routinized in religiously aesthetic practices.

There is value of a certain type in religious admiration. It is better to respect Christ than to despise Him; better to praise than to curse Him. However, admiration must not be made an end in the religious life. Every Christian must go beyond admiration of Christ; he must have more than a deferential respect for the Christian way of life. Religion, as loyalty, must be demonstrated in actual life. Josiah Royce says that loyalty "is complete only in motor terms, never merely in sentimental terms. It is useless to call my feelings loyal unless my muscles somehow express this loyalty."[4]

LOVE THAT MOTIVATES

When the Christians began to preach their Gospel to the world they found that their concept of love was too big for the Greek language, rich as the language was. Indeed,

[4]Josiah Royce, *Race Questions, Provincialism, and Other American Problems* (New York: Macmillan, 1908), p. 239.

the Greeks had several words for love but all of them were too small. To solve this problem, the early believers took a potentially large word, *agape,* and imbued it with added meaning. The word became born again and it served as the basic term for Christian love, being used about 250 times in the New Testament.

Christian love has both emotional and rational elements. It has both emotional warmth and rational esteem. The word *agape* emphasizes the rational and volitional aspects of love, as well as the emotional elements. Christian love includes the whole personality. Jesus commanded men to love God with all the heart (the center of affections) and with all the mind (the center of rational and volitional life). This is total love (Mark 12:30).

Christian love, *agape,* is a divine gift to the believer. It is the result of God's presence in the human heart. "The love of God is shed abroad in our hearts by the Holy Ghost which is given unto us" (Romans 5:5b). *Agape* is divine love expressing itself through human life because God dwells within. One cannot have God's presence in life without manifesting divine love. "God is love" (I John 4:8b).

Christian love fosters spiritual growth because it frees the human personality from destructive dispositions. There is "an expulsive power in a new affection." Paul believed that love cast out impatience by its own patience and kindness; expelled jealousy by its own spirit of humility; and did away with irritability and resentment by its own generosity (I Corinthians 13:4-6).

The love of God in the human heart provides a spiritual climate in which the Christian life matures. The warmth of divine love gives rise to religious ideals; it fosters the development of healthful ethics; and it brings about maturity in Christian service.

Many secular psychotherapists emphasize the importance of love on the human level, apart from religion. They believe that love is essential for a healthful development of human personality, recognizing that genuine love is one of the basic needs of persons. Harry Stack Sullivan, for instance, says that one must experience "the quiet miracle" of being loved and of loving in return if one is to achieve his true potential. Psychotherapists recognize also the healing power of love for maladjusted persons. Eric Fromm states that analytic theory is essentially an attempt to help the patient gain or regain his capacity for love. This means "ability to love productively, to love without greed, without submission or domination, to love from the fulness of the personality."[5] Without "the quiet miracle" of love, ideals never appear, ethics become unhealthful, and service becomes selfish.

Divine love pervades the atmosphere in the birth of spiritual *objectives*. Ideals become the guiding images and the master passions of life. Ideals germinate and grow in the seedbed of cherished interests. The things we esteem give direction to our lives. Moreover, dynamic love enlists rational and emotional elements in personality that provide the driving force for the achievement of the objectives.

Divine love provides the motive power for Christian *ethics*. "The moral ideal for Christians lies not in a code, not in a social order. It lies in a life where love of God and man is the main spring of every thought, and word, and action."[6] Psychiatry agrees with religion that ethics must be motivated by love. If the moral life is not so motivated it is unhealthful and immature.

Dynamic Christian love fosters healthful ethical development because it provides a basis for interior morality. The motivation to do right springs from the heart and not from an external code or from some compelling circumstance in

[5]Eric Fromm, *Psycholanalysis and Religion* (Yale University Press, 1950), p. 87.
[6]T. W. Manson, *The Teaching of Jesus* (New York: Cambridge University Press, 1932), p. 312.

environment. External morality is superficial. It is static; one does not grow ethically by the arbitrary keeping of rules. Morality by prescription is always an immature morality. It is rooted in servitude and not in spontaneity. It is compulsive and not creative. Rule-keeping is frustrating; an ethical life that springs from love is fulfilling. Interior love of righteousness frees one, as Karen Horney said, "from the tyranny of the shoulds."

Moreover, sometimes external morality is actually harmful. It frequently gives rise to unhealthful guilt feelings. The rule-keepers are never able to keep all of the precepts of an exterior code and they feel guilty when they fail. The situation is more favorable with love-motivated ethics. The man who lives by love knows that his love for God remains constant though he unwittingly failed to reach all of his ideals.

Dynamic Christian love also provides a basis for a personally-authenticated ethical life. Psychiatrists point out that much morality is an unconscious morality. This comes about from a strong prohibitive conscience, the super ego, which is the result of the uncritical acceptance of the ethical patterns of one's early environment. The adult who has large areas of unconscious morality in his life has never thought through the bases of his ethics. He has never personalized his moral life. He lives, in part, on the basis of inhibitions that are rooted in childhood experiences. He is compulsive about keeping certain rules, fearing that some dreadful thing may happen to him if he does not do so.

Christian love, with its large rational elements, motivates one to live a thoughtful and intelligent ethical life. One looks at the earlier pattern of life and validates all that is relevant and true. He then lives on the basis of his own convictions. He adapts ethical principles to unique situations in life. He does more than observe tidbits of morality. Ethical principles become pervasive in all of his life. Dynamic love leads him to Christian maturity.

Moreover, dynamic Christian love provides a basis for Christian *service*. Dynamic Christian love goes beyond admiration. In reference to persons, admiration takes delight in those who are already admirable; it rejoices in those who are lovely; it esteems the noble. Christian love does more than this. It esteems the unlovely; it goes out to those whose lives have been marred by sin and tragedy; it looks beyond what a man is presently to what he is potentially. This is the expression of God's love to others through redeemed personalities.

Christian love imbues every act of kindly service with a spiritual magnetism that makes the deed attractive. Paul makes it clear that genuine love has no substitute. He says that great personal sacrifice, even the giving of one's body to be burned, is an exercise in futility if one does not have love (I Corinthians 13:3). He also says that, in the book of spiritual mathematics, the gift of preaching, plus extraordinary knowledge, plus mountain-moving faith, adds up to a cipher if one does not have real love (I Corinthians 13:2). The answer is zero in every equation of benevolent service if love is not there.

Acts of mercy become offensive to the recipient if he cannot intuit that they were motivated by love. He is inwardly repelled by them, though he accepts the gratuities, because he senses that they arose out of pity, or out of a desire on the part of his benefactor to aggrandize self by expressing a self-assumed superiority.

On the other hand, dynamic Christian love gives deeds of helpfulness an inner magnetism. Love does kindly deeds with a genius and aptness, keeping self in the background. It goes the second mile with a glad spirit. It does gracious deeds of which the rule-makers never thought. It gives every deed an aura of beauty, as perfume in the flowers.

Theologians sometimes have made a useful distinction between complacent love and benevolent love. Complacent love is rooted in admiration and approval. It represents a static kind of good will; a tranquil pleasure or satisfaction in an object or a person. On the other hand, benevolent love is active and dynamic. It represents a disposition to do good and to promote the happiness of others. This disposition extends to both God and man in the Christian religion. Divinely given love is the motivating center *par excellence* of the Christian's life. It represents the genius of the Christian's faith, setting its mark on everything he does. Maturity in the Christian life is measured in terms of maturity of love. Love is the sovereign value of the spiritual life.

BIBLIOGRAPHY

Allport, Gordon W., *Becoming: Basic Considerations for a Psychology of Personality*. New Haven: Yale University Press, 1955.

................, *Personality, a Psychological Interpretation*, New York: Henry Holt and Co., 1937.

................, *The Individual and His Religion*. New York: The Macmillan Co., 1950.

Ames, Edward Scribner, *The Psychology of Religious Experience*. Boston: Houghton Mifflin Co., 1910.

Ansbacher, Heinz L., and Ansbacher, Rowena R., *The Individual Psychology of Alfred Adler*. New York: Basic Books, 1956.

Asch, Solomon E., *Social Psychology*. New York: Prentice-Hall, 1952. 1952).

Augustine, Saint, *Confessions;* translated by J. G. Pilkington. New York: Boni and Liveright, 1927.

Barbour, Clifford E., *Sin and the New Psychology*. New York: The Abingdon Press, 1930.

Begbie, Harold, *More Twice-Born Men*. New York: G. P. Putnam's Sons, 1923.

................, *Twice-Born Men*. New York: Fleming H. Revell Co., 1909.

Boisen, Anton T., *The Exploration of the Inner World*. New York: Harper & Brothers, 1936.

Bonthius, Robert H., *Christian Pathways to Self Assurance*. New York: King's Crown Press, 1948.

Brown, T. E., "Indwelling" in *The Collected Poems* of T. E. Brown. London: The Macmillan Co., 1900.

Clark, Elmer T., *The Psychology of Religious Awakening*. New York: The Macmillan Co., 1929.

Clark, Walter Houston, *The Psychology of Religion*. New York: The Macmillan Co., 1958.

Coe, George Albert, *The Psychology of Religion*. Chicago: University of Chicago Press, 1916.

Conklin, Edmond S., *The Psychology of Religious Adjustment*. New York: The Macmillan Co., 1929.

Fox, George, *Journal;* Revised edition by J. L. Nickalls. Cambridge (Eng.): Cambridge University Press, 1952.

Fromm, Erich, *Man For Himself*. New York: Rinehart & Co., Inc., 1947.

..............., *Psychoanalysis and Religion*. New Haven: Yale University Press, 1950.

Goldbrunner, Josef, *Holiness Is Wholeness*. New York: Pantheon, 1955.

Goldstein, Kurt, *The Organism: A Holistic Approach to Biology Derived from Pathological Data in Man*. New York: American Book Co., 1939.

Hadfield, J. A., *Psychology and Morals*. New York: R. M. McBride & Company.

Harkness, Georgia, *The Dark Night of the Soul*. New York and Nashville: Abingdon-Cokesbury, 1945.

Heiler, Friedrich, *Prayer: A Study in the History and the Psychology of Religion;* translated and edited by Samuel McComb. New York: Oxford University Press, Inc., 1932.

Henzie, Leland E. and Robert J. Campbell, *Psychiatric Dictionary* New York: Oxford University Press, 1953.

Hocking, William Ernest, *The Meaning of God in Human Experience*. New Haven: Yale University Press, 1924.

Horney, Karen, *The Neurotic Personality of Our Time*. New York: W. W. Norton and Co., 1937.

James, William, *Varieties of Religious Experience*. New York: Modern Library, 1902.

Johnson, Paul E., *Christian Love*. New York and Nashville: Abingdon-Cokesbury, 1951.

..............., *Psychology of Religion*. New York and Nashville: Abingdon-Cokesbury, 1959.

Jones, E. Stanley, *Victorious Living*. New York: Abingdon, 1936.

Josey, C. C., *The Psychology of Religion*. New York: The Macmillan Co., 1927.

Jung, Carl G., *Modern Man in Search of a Soul*. London: K. Paul, Trench, Trubner & Co., Ltd., 1933.

Kierkegaard, Soren, *Either — Or*. Princeton: Princeton University Press, 1944.

..............., *The Concept of Dread*. Princeton: Princeton University Press, 1944.

..............., *The Sickness Unto Death*. Princeton: Princeton University Press, 1941.

..............., *Training in Christianity*. Princeton: Princeton University Press, 1941.

Leuba, James H., *A. Psychological Study of Religion*. New York: The Macmillan Co., 1912.

..............., *The Psychology of Religious Mysticism*. New York: Harcourt, Brace & Co., 1925.

Ligon, Ernest M., *The Psychology of Christian Personality*. New York: The Macmillan Co., 1936.

Lynd, Robert, *Dr. Johnson and Company*. Garden City: Doubleday, Doran and Co., 1928.

Manson, T. W., *The Teaching of Jesus*. New York: Cambridge University, 1932.

Marston, Leslie R., *From Chaos to Character*. Winona Lake, Indiana: Light and Life Press, 1937.

Maslow, A. H., *Motivation and Personality*. New York: Harper and Brothers, 1954.

Mavis, W. Curry, *Beyond Conformity*. Winona Lake, Ind.: Light and Life Press, 1958.

May, Rollo, *The Meaning of Anxiety*. New York: The Ronald Press Company, 1950.

McKenzie, John G., *Nervous Disorders and Religion; A Study of Souls in the Making*. London: Allen and Unwin, Ltd., 1951.

Mowrer, Hobart, *Learning Theory and Personality Dynamics*. New York: The Ronald Press Company, 1950.

Murray, James A. H., *A New English Dictionary on Historical Principles*. Oxford: Clarendon Press, 1901.

Outler, Albert C., *Psychotherapy and the Christian Message*. New York: Harper and Brothers, 1954.

Pratt, James B., *The Psychology of Religious Belief*. New York: The Macmillan Co., 1907.

..............., *The Religious Consciousness: A Psychological Study*. New York: The Macmillan Co., 1920.

Roberts, David E., *Psychotherapy and a Christian View of Man*. New York: Charles Scribner's Sons, 1950.

Royce, Josiah, *Race Questions, Provincialism, and Other American Problems*. New York: The Macmillan Co., 1908.

Ruch, Floyd, *Psychology and Life*. Chicago: Scott, Foresman and Co., 1953.

Sorokin, P. A., *The Crisis of Our Age*. New York: E. P. Dutton & Co., Inc., 1941.

Starbuck, Edwin Diller, *The Psychology of Religion;* 3rd edition. New York: Charles Scribner's Sons, 1912.

Stratton, George M., *Psychology of the Religious Life*. London: George Allen & Co., Ltd., 1911.

Strunk, Orlo, Sr., *Religion, A Psychological Interpretation*. New York: Abingdon, 1962.

Strunk, Orlo Jr., *Readings in Psychology of Religion*. New York: Abingdon Press, 1959.

Thouless, Robert H., *An Introduction to the Psychology of Religion*. Cambridge: Cambridge University Press, 1923.

Tillich, Paul, *The Courage To Be*. New Haven: Yale University Press, 1952.

................, *The New Being*. New York: Charles Scribner's Sons, 1955.

Tournier, Paul, *A Doctor's Casebook in the Light of the Bible*. London: S.C.M. Press, 1954.

Weatherhead, Leslie D., *Psychology, Religion, and Healing*. New York and Nashville: Abingdon-Cokesbury, 1951.

White, Ernest, *Christian Life and the Unconscious*. New York: Harper and Brothers, 1955.

Zweig, Stephan, *The Living Thoughts of Tolstoi*. New York: Longmans, Green & Company.

INDEX

Abdul-Haqq, Akbar, 25
Adjustment, 64-66
Adler, Alfred, 31, 36-37
Admirers of Christ, 139-142
Agape, 143
Aggression, 67
Allport, Gordon, 29, 48
Ambivalence, 19, 39, 87, 141
Anxiety, 27, 44, 120
Approach — Avoidance impulses, 18
Asch, Solomon E., 30
Aspiration, 101-104
Assurance, 44-55
Attitudes, 30, 48, 96, 113, 128-131
Augustine, 22
Authority complex, 59

Barbour, C. E., 112
Behaviorism, 96, 97
Bergson, Henri, 59
Bible, 82-86, 124, 125, 133, 134
Bonthius, R. H., 50
Boswell, James, 140, 141
Brown, T. E., 41, 42
Brunner, Emil, 108
Bunyan, John, 26

Cambridge Platonists, 139
Carnal nature, 60, 61
Chalmers, Thomas, 37
Christian service, 146
Cleansing, spiritual, 37-43
Clement of Alexandria, 92
Coleman, J. M., 124
Compensation, 12, 13
Complex, psychological, 59
Conditioned commitment, 17
Conditioned reflexes, 97
Constitutional factors, 72-76
Conversion, 24-33, 35
Counseling, 135, 136

David, King, 83
Darwin, C., 108
Defoe, Daniel, 116

Deists, 121, 122
Depression, 76, 77
Depth psychology, 97
Discipline, 130
Divine creativity, 24-33
Drummond, Henry, 131, 132
Dynamics, spiritual, 111

Ego-enhancement, 64
Eliot, George, 79
Eliot, T. S., 54, 101
Estrangement, sense of, 49, 50
Ethics, Christian, 144

Faith, 94-95, 118-127
Family worship, 90
Forgiveness, 26, 121
Freud, S., 108
Fromm, Eric, 144
Frustration tolerance, 73
Frustration, spiritual, 73-81
Futility, sense of, 53-55, 71

God's will, 130, 131
Goethe, 17
Gnostic movement, 74
Goldbrunner, Josef, 100
Goldstein, Kurt, 34
Gray, David, 11
Group dynamics, 89
Guidance, divine, 128-138
Guilt feelings, 26, 27, 44, 52, 67, 71,
   120
Guilt-ridden piety, 27

Hadfield, J. A., 20
Health, 77
Holy Spirit, 40, 41, 42, 46, 47, 63, 69-
   71, 100, 126
Horney, Karen, 52, 145
Hostility, 49-52
Hugo, Victor, 137

Id, 78, 97
Ideals, secular, 112

Ideals, spiritual, 113, 144
Identification, 13, 14
Inferiority feelings, 44, 59
Innate goodness, 21
Interests, 32, 48, 111, 112
Isaiah, 50

James, the apostle, 39, 79
James, William, 28
Jeremiah, the prophet, 86
Jesus, 25, 31, 36, 40, 69, 76, 78, 80, 86, 94, 104, 109, 110, 114, 123, 126, 141
John, the apostle, 39
Jones, E. Stanley, 44
Jung, Carl, 22, 23, 54, 55

Kierkegaard, S., 35, 37, 52, 66, 103, 114, 115, 139, 140, 142
Kipling, R., 137, 138

Larwell, Gordon, 64-66
Lewis, C. S., 36
Lindbergh, Anne Morrow, 100
Love
  Benevolent, 147
  Christian, 143-147
  Complacent, 146, 147
Lowell, J. R., 79, 141
Lynd, Robert, 140

Maladjustive impulses, 59-72
Manson, H. W., 144
Marston, Leslie R., 77
Marx, Karl, 108
Mary Magdalene, 31
Maslow, A. H., 34
Masochistic impulse, 67, 120, 121
Methodists, 89
Milton, John, 142
Moberly, Walter, 108
Moravians, 89
More, Hannah, 114
Motivation, 29, 60, 62
Mowrer, Hobart, 26
Mozley, J. B., 101
Mueller, George, 126
Munger, T. T., 102

Neurosis, 26, 120
Nietzsche, F., 108

Original sin, 60, 61
Outler, Albert C., 20, 21

Paul, the apostle, 17, 24, 25, 28, 31, 42, 43, 47, 53, 63, 78, 80, 81, 83, 91, 93, 95, 109, 132, 143, 146
Personal fulfillment, 34, 35
Peter the apostle, 39, 79, 80, 86
Pharisees, 13, 14, 19
Phillips, J. B., 43
Pilgrim's Progress, 18, 22
Praise, 91-93
Pratt, J. B., 30
Prayer, 90-95, 135
Psychoanalysis, 97

Rationalization, 66
Regeneration, spiritual, 46, 47
Repression, 59
Resistance, psychic, 70
Royce, Josiah, 142
Ruch, Floyd, 14

Sacrifice, personal, 93
Sanctification, 38-43
Saul, King, 50, 51, 83
Saul of Tarsus, 14
Schleiermacher, F., 128
Secularism, 107-117
Seeley, J. R., 101
Selective perception, 110, 111
Self actualization, 34, 35
Seneca, 18
Sentiments, 29, 48
Sincerity, 98-101
Small groups, 88, 89
Sociology, 98
Sonship, sense of, 47
Spiritual fixation, 35
Spiritual maturity, 36, 37
Starbuck, E. D., 31
Stein, Gertrude, 53
Stekel, W., 19, 52
Sullivan, H. S., 144
Super ego, 145
Symbol-substitutes, 15

Talbert, Ernest L., 85
Taylor, Harry Milton, 11
Temperament, 75, 76, 118, 119
  choleric, 76
  melancholic, 76, 119
  phlegmatic, 75, 76
  sanguine, 76

Temptation, 78-81
Thomas, the apostle, 41
Tillich, Paul, 51

Tolstoi, Leo, 53, 54
Tournier, Paul, 85
Toynbee, Arnold, 111

Unconscious, 60
Unconscious morality, 145

Values, inverted, 114-117

Wesley, John, 45, 49, 55
Wesley, Samuel, 55
Wheatley, Melvin E., 37
White, Ernest, 55
Worship, 71, 86, 125

Zaccheus, 31